The Call to the Desert

A Spiritual Journey of Love, Understanding
and Compassion

Joanne Hutchinson

BALBOA.
PRESS
A DIVISION OF HAY HOUSE

Balboa Press books may be ordered through booksellers or by contacting:

Balboa Press
A Division of Hay House
1663 Liberty Drive
Bloomington, IN 47403
www.balboapress.com
1-(877) 407-4847

Because of the dynamic nature of the Internet, any web addresses or links contained in this book may have changed since publication and may no longer be valid. The views expressed in this work are solely those of the author and do not necessarily reflect the views of the publisher, and the publisher hereby disclaims any responsibility for them.

The author of this book does not dispense medical advice or prescribe the use of any technique as a form of treatment for physical, emotional, or medical problems without the advice of a physician, either directly or indirectly. The intent of the author is only to offer information of a general nature to help you in your quest for emotional and spiritual well-being. In the event you use any of the information in this book for yourself, which is your constitutional right, the author and the publisher assume no responsibility for your actions.

Any people depicted in stock imagery provided by Thinkstock are models, and such images are being used for illustrative purposes only.
Certain stock imagery © Thinkstock.

ISBN: 978-1-4525-0158-1 (sc)
ISBN: 978-1-4525-0160-4 (dj)
ISBN: 978-1-4525-0159-8 (e)

Library of Congress Control Number: 2010918085
Printed in the United States of America

WestBow Press rev. date: 1/31/2011

This book is dedicated to all those who choose to live life with purpose and for the greater and higher good of all.

Gratitude

I would like to give my thanks and heart felt gratitude to Valinda Fletcher, Jenny Fraser, Mary Bird, Somesh Eladchumanar, Mouna Desai, Odette Raven, Eunice Warne, Peta Thompson, Scott Travis, Julia Wei, Lauryn Buchanan and Hannah Talbot for the generous contributions of clothing and art materials that we gifted to so many children in Egypt. Thank you for your ongoing love and support. From these first steps, it has now grown into something more significant as we continue to work together to change lives.

Thank you Somesh Eladchumanar for helping me to complete this book and for your honest feedback. And to Di Maxwell at Creativedge who provided me with significant help and assistance in the design and production of this book.

And a special thank you to Elizabeth Meadows, Mum, Nana and my daughter Hannah for your ongoing love and encouragement in my life and work.

Authors Note:

Out of respect to the people I met in Egypt, all names have been changed to preserve their privacy. All information in this book is written from my personal perspective.

Contents

Chapter 1

GETTING TO EGYPT

It was Sunday the 11th of October 2009 and I was excited to be heading to the airport for my flight from Auckland to Cairo. I knew my bags were over the 20kg allowance as I had been collecting children's clothes and art supplies to gift to some children living in poverty in a village in Giza. And wow, the generosity of my friends and clients was so amazing that I had problems fitting it all into my suitcase.

I arrived at the airport and went to the check in counter. My large suitcase was over the baggage limit but the staff were not concerned about that. What they were more interested in was my hand luggage which they asked me to show them and then said they needed to check the weight. It was 10kg and the allowance was just 7kg so I was then asked to re-pack it to meet the requirement. It was a funny feeling as I wondered how on earth I could fit more stuff into the bigger suitcase which frankly was full and was the reason why I had more hand luggage than I would normally travel with. I decided I couldn't leave anything behind and I just had to make it fit so there I was in the middle of an international airport, kneeling on my suitcase squashing and forcing everything in until I got it zipped up which I did. I was completely oblivious to everyone around me and in hindsight; it must have looked hilariously funny.

It was now over 27kg and I wondered if I would be charged for excess baggage but luck was on my side and they let it go through. That was a relief. I then headed to Immigration where they also checked the weight of my carry on luggage which surprisingly weighed more than at the check in (something to be said about the calibration of weighing machines) but it was just under the limit. Phew! By now, I decided that there were some things I needed to learn from this to apply to my future trips.

I made my way to the departure gate and waited for the boarding call. This didn't happen at the designated time and I could see the level of anxiety increasing amongst my fellow travelers. At last a boarding call was made, only to learn that boarding had been delayed for thirty minutes. Now that everyone had been informed, there was a collective sigh of relief that we now knew what was happening. Thirty minutes later, we were told there was a further delay and the next message was that due to mechanical problems with the engine, boarding was now expected to be delayed for a further two hours.

The vast majority of passengers verbalized their frustration with loud sighs, indignation and anger – all at the same time. It was so perfectly synchronized while the staff graciously offered free food and drinks. I found it amusing to observe the group dynamics but my grin was not welcomed. Of course, it was for our safety that the plane was being fixed on the ground but unfortunately this point was lost on most people. Watching the group behavior, I thought this is a great example of the term "collective consciousness".

I went for a walk to the bookshop to buy a highlighter pen and when I returned I felt thirsty. The idea of an orange juice sounded perfect. I poured a glass of orange juice and went to sit down, delicately balancing my hand luggage when my handbag slipped off my shoulder knocking the orange juice directly onto my lap.

I now had orange juice all over my white pants. Now it was an interesting thing that just a few days ago, I was telling a friend of mine that white clothes are generally not the best color to travel in. So why did I choose to wear white clothes today? What a great look, I thought! I laughed and headed to the bathroom for some emergency washing, entertaining an elderly lady who saw the funny side of my accident and we both roared with laughter given the fact that I hadn't even left New Zealand (NZ) yet. I wondered what state I would be in by the time I reached Cairo some 24 hours later. I returned to the waiting area still with wet pants but now mostly white again and I secretly hoped that no-one would notice.

Fortunately, the rest of the trip was uneventful and I arrived in awe of the new Cairo International Airport, such a different experience to the old terminal which was like landing at an airport in the dark ages. This airport was impressive and I wondered how much money it must have cost and how this was balanced with the social issues in Egypt and all those who live in poverty.

As I waited for my luggage, I became mesmerized by the new technology of the baggage carousels. Instead of all the bags coming out at once and crashing into each other, each bag patiently waited its turn until there was a clear space before advancing to the carousel. How innovative I thought. Whoever developed this technology had really thought this through and it was quite amazing.

With my bags in tow and an airport guide, my next stop was to change some American dollars to Egyptian pounds before we left there. We approached one of the banks and I was pleasantly surprised to find the rate at the airport was very good. From experience, I knew to carry lots of small denominations as Egypt is essentially a cash society and it can be hard to get change. They had plenty of small notes and so they gave me plenty. I thought that this was great and we then walked towards Customs. I was halfway there when a man came running after me. It seemed I had left my passport at the bank. I am not sure how I managed to do that but I did.

A rather large queue had developed at Customs. There was a lot of pushing and shoving going on when two men started a verbal fight in a language that I presumed was Arabic. The Customs Officer exerted his power by turning his back on the two men fighting and deciding that the queue started on the opposite side to where they were, which was also where I was standing. He ignored my guide's pleas to let me through, so we patiently waited. My guide was adamant I would be through in a jiff and without any hassle. This is, of course his job and he is an expert at it. Then there was another exchange in Arabic and suddenly the gate was opened for me and I was whisked through without the need for a baggage search. I said thank you to the Customs Officer and wondered what my guide had said. I was curious to know what those magic words were.

Outside of the airport, I was introduced to my driver and a new guide, Ahmed who would take me to the hotel. By now, it was just after 6am and there was no traffic to speak of. Although I had been traveling for 24 hours, I realized that these men had also had an early start and wondered what time their day had started and more importantly, what time would they finish? We arrived at the hotel just before 7am and Ahmed asked Reception for my room, knowing the rule that check in is strictly at noon. We were told to wait until after 7am and try again which we did, but still had no luck.

While we waited, we talked about Egypt in general and the places I would be visiting. There is something like four million cars in Egypt of which they say there are about two million cars are on the streets of Cairo and about twenty million people live here. It is a very big and busy city with traffic congestion and the black air one of many issues.

The public schools typically have one teacher to one hundred students and around one lecturer to one thousand students at university. The fees are very cheap around US$20 and US$40 respectively for a year. There is of course private education where the student teacher ratios are more in line with what you would see in the Western world and these cost a lot more.

I asked Ahmed for some advice on tipping. Tipping is not a custom in NZ and so it is easy to forget to do. Here though, the salaries are very low and most people depend on the tips to supplement their income. Many people live on about 400 Egyptian pounds (EGP) per month which is about US$80.

I had a meeting with the New Zealand Embassy the next day and Ahmed told me that the taxi fare should be about 10 Egyptian pounds and showed me the exit from the hotel that would be the best one to use. He said it was very safe around here and with the Nile directly across the road, there were always plenty of people around. He also gave me some advice that later turned out to be quite profound. He said "there are many people who will want to help you, but many of them will have their own interests at heart. You will need to be careful". I understood this to be about discernment and throughout my trip; these words often would come back to me when things went wrong.

The Egyptians find it unusual for women to be single and traveling on their own so you can become a target for things you don't need. Men often project fear onto you that you are not safe to be by yourself and therefore you need them to accompany you, always at a cost of course.

We waited some more and then Ahmed suggested that I go and ask for my room. Typically Reception is staffed by men so I found it unusual to see a stunning young lady behind the counter who came to serve me.

I noticed that she kept looking at me out of the corner of her eye while she was checking me in. She had a radiant smile and a mischievous look. Ahmed and I thought we were just doing the paperwork so I could check in at noon but voila, a miracle happened. Not only did I get my room, she gave me an upgrade and my room number was 911 – a spiritually significant number! I was so excited that I jumped with joy and turned to thank Ahmed for his help. When I turned back to thank the lady, she was gone. She was like a mysterious beautiful goddess, appearing from nowhere to help me and when this was done, she mysteriously vanished.

The bellman helped me with my bags to my room. At last I thought, I am here and it feels so good. I knew I was home.

I took a shower and put on some fresh clothes and all traces of jet lag seemed to disappear. I decided to have some breakfast and then contemplated what I would do today. I wanted to visit the Cairo Museum but I had to cross the road first and you have to be in Egypt to understand what this means. It's not just one road, it's like a couple of highways and although there are pedestrian crossings, drivers have the right of way and lanes and lines don't mean anything.

I remembered Ahmed's words when I asked him where the museum was. He said "the museum is opposite the hotel" and showed me where (in fact, I could see it from the balcony in my room) and with laughter in his voice he said, "you only have to cross the road". Yes, I thought, you only have to cross the road. It sounds so easy but how do you cross the road here?

As I was contemplating this, I felt a twinge of tiredness and thought I'd lie on the bed for a few minutes and think about how I would do this. That was about 10am. I fell asleep and in my jet-lagged and comatose state, I remember being lucid enough to answer the door when Housekeeping arrived and then went straight back to sleep again. When I finally woke up, it was 5pm. So much for visiting the Museum today!

By now it was peak hour traffic in Cairo and it was intoxicatingly chaotic. I had to go out to the balcony to take a look. In every direction, it's a constant stream of cars, lights and noise. Cars constantly toot their horns to communicate to the other drivers that are about an inch away on either side of them so they know that you are there. And then there is the "call to prayer" that bellows out from the mosques. It is so incredibly different to where I live.

I went back inside and decided it was time for dinner. There were many restaurants to choose from and I found an Indian restaurant that looked perfect. It opened at 7pm and there was just me and a group of four retired English tourists who had been here a few days. I overheard them saying they were picking up their rental car tomorrow and wondered how they would survive the Cairo traffic. Driving here is an art and certainly not for the faint-hearted.

With so few of us at dinner, we were spoilt for service and the food was magnificent. They offered fragrant hand towels at the beginning and end of the meal, a complimentary assortment of starters and condiments to complete the meal. It was all delivered with such grace and gratitude that you couldn't help but feel like you were royalty. The service was so impeccable that it reminded me of the principle that giving and receiving need to be in balance. "Give first" is such a great business practice.

I returned to my room and went out to the balcony to see what the traffic was like now. Closing the door behind me, I noticed how black and smoky the air was and I really thought that someone had just lit a fire below me. I realized it was the pollution from the cars and with no wind, it just sits there. I was surprised how bad it was. It seemed much worse than I remembered. I wondered how anyone can breathe here. And does anyone care? I felt certain this must be beyond the World Health safety limits and not surprisingly breathing related illnesses including cancer are one of the highest causes of death here which sadly could be prevented.

Keen to go back inside, my heart missed several beats and the adrenalin pumped through me when I realized I had locked myself out. I felt an overwhelming sense of fear and panic. My mind filled with thoughts as to how stupid I must be to have done this and what do I do now? Would I be sleeping on the balcony waiting for Housekeeping to come knocking on my door to rescue me tomorrow? What time would they come? "Oh boy, I thought, this is not good".

With what felt like an eternity, I sensed that I needed to try the door once more and then found a small sign that said push this button to unlock the door and to my great relief, it worked and I was inside again. Still shaking and in shock, I decided I needed some Rescue Remedy.

After that, I decided to go to bed. It was the finish to my very long day to get here and the start of my Egyptian adventure.

Chapter 2

OUT AND ABOUT IN CAIRO

My meeting with the NZ Embassy was at 11am. I knew I had plenty of time so I chose to take my time getting out of bed today. I took a shower and after I had switched the water off, I could hear Housekeeping knocking on the door, a few doors down from mine. It wasn't yet 8.30 in the morning and I thought surely they are not coming to service the rooms now.

To be on the safe side, I decided my priority was to get dressed and I am glad I did. In less than five minutes, the knock was at my door and when I opened it, I was greeted by a very young smiling man who bellowed "Housekeeping – I have come to clean your room". I was dressed but my hair was still wet and I had no make-up on and I thought, I'm not ready yet and so I asked him to come back in five minutes. He said "five minutes" and I said yes, "I need to dry my hair". "Five minutes", he said again. I nodded, he smiled and left.

I went down for breakfast. This was a very large and busy hotel that also catered for conferences and it seemed like there were a few on. Consequently, the restaurant was extremely busy and each time I went to get food from the buffet, I would return to find I had lost my table. It was like playing the game 'musical chairs'.

I never eat fried eggs at home but there was something wonderful about having them cooked in front of you. The chefs enjoy entertaining and love to flip the eggs and omelets to demonstrate their skills and their prowess usually with a little smirk on their faces. And so I stood in line, asked for my two fried eggs which was the start of a seriously bad habit. Later I discovered the pancakes and had these too!

One of the great things about this restaurant is that it looked out onto the Nile. The view is to die for. I loved it and could sit here for hours just watching and enjoying the world go by. There is always so much activity here, day and night.

I went back to my room, surprised to find that Housekeeping had not been yet. It seemed odd that there was such a sense of urgency to clean my room at 8.30am and then nothing. I left a tip in the bathroom and went down to the lobby.

It was time to get a taxi to the Embassy. I had been told it was an easy five minute drive depending on the traffic! As I left the Hotel, I found the bellman who was dressed in a very bright red jacket with shiny gold buttons. He spoke very good English and I explained where I wanted to go. Taxis came past and he waved them on. He said I will arrange a hotel car for you for fifty pound. I remembered that Ahmed had told me it would be about ten pound, so I said that it was too much. That started another discussion. He said "no, fifty pound, air-conditioned car, not like taxi and your own driver, he wait for you" and he ushered the driver and another man over. There was some more discussion and then I said "all right then, let's go".

The car was parked across the road from the hotel. We had to walk past the booth for the Tourism Police. There are Tourism Police everywhere and it is one of the main reasons why it is so safe to travel in Egypt. They take complaints seriously. The Tourism Policeman saw me about to leave with these men and immediately stopped us to ask where I was going. The bellman spoke to him in Arabic and I spoke to him in English. He said OK and waved us on. I liked the idea that someone else was checking on where I was going and who I was going with.

Crossing the road was easy. To my surprise, the bellman and the driver stood on the road with their hands in the stop sign position, acting as traffic police to stop the cars and motorbikes to let me cross. I laughed; it was like being the Queen of England.

Once in the car, I realized that my driver spoke very little English. He was a quiet, unassuming older man and I liked him. He felt genuine. And I hoped he knew where we were going. Just in case he didn't, I kept an eye on the buildings that we were passing.

He found the building which had both a North Tower and a South Tower. I needed to go to the North Tower and he had driven into the South Tower entrance. I tried to explain this to him but he didn't understand. I showed him the address, pointed to the words in English on the building and realized he couldn't read English. No problem I thought, I will find it.

Being a prominent building with embassies, there were many security staff including the German Shepherd guard dogs. The car was checked by the guards for bombs and I realized that my driver was nervous and not so sure of himself. He had lost his confidence and this seemed to add to the confusion. We were told to park in the underground car park and he stopped to drop me off at the entrance to the South Tower. I wasn't sure how long I would be so I said I would meet him back here, at this spot at 12 o'clock and he said he would wait for me. He then drove off but I wasn't convinced that he had understood what I had said but I thought I'd have to deal with that later. First I must get to this meeting.

I walked over to the security guard sitting at the entrance to the South Tower. I told him where I wanted to go and showed him the address. He was very understanding but couldn't understand my English. It was the lady sitting next to him that pointed to the direction that I needed to take which essentially was the other end of the car park. Off I trotted with my address clutched in my hand, confident that I knew where I was going.

I found the North Tower entrance and spoke to the security staff who told me to take the elevator to the 1st floor. Thinking I was now in the North Tower, I was surprised to find myself in a modern shopping mall. I knew this was not right and found another person to ask for more instructions.

It seemed that North Tower was just next door.

I was finally there. It was 11am and I was on time. Perfect.

The New Zealand Embassy is impressive with some of the nicest offices I have seen even by NZ standards. It had a very corporate feel and I immediately jumped into my corporate mode. I was greeted by a familiar face in the foyer, a photo of John Key, the current Prime Minister.

The Embassy was set up about three years ago and I learnt that in the Second World War, we had thousands of troops who fought in El Alamein to secure Egypt from the German invasion. Today, there are around 200 New Zealanders living in Cairo and the Embassy had set up a networking group called KICs - 'Kiwis in Cairo' and another group called TICs - 'Teachers in Cairo'. I thought this was a great idea.

The purpose of my visit to the Embassy was to ask for their advice and help to find an orphanage and possibly an animal care charity that I could visit, with the view of building a long term relationship with them so that when I come back each year, I can bring resources that contribute to improving the quality of life. 'Giving back' is one of my core beliefs and a foundational principle in my businesses.

The Ambassador's Office is parallel to the river Nile so the view is sensational and it looked out to the Pyramids. The Commissioner sat opposite me which meant that the Pyramids were behind him. As I talked with him, I could see these wonderful rainbow colors moving and dancing magically around the Pyramids. They were very playful and I knew they were my spiritual guides calling to me and welcoming me home. It was hard to keep focused and not be distracted by them. Yes, I thought, Egypt is my spiritual home and I am home. The energies are strong and powerful here and I see and feel the most amazing things. I couldn't wait to go to the Pyramids in a few days time.

When I left the Embassy, I returned to the spot where my driver had left me. It was 11.45am and I waited for him. The basement car park was full of expensive cars, BMW's, Mercedes and the like. It was a rare sight because the average car is very old here. I waited and waited and one of the security guards became concerned for me. He couldn't understand my English and I couldn't understand his Arabic and I thought I must learn some Arabic. I told him I was OK and he gestured to his mobile phone wanting to ring someone for me. I didn't have the driver's number and it was only just past noon so I said I was OK waiting.

After five more minutes had passed, he was still concerned for me that he went out of his way to find me someone who could speak English and brought them over to speak with me. I explained that I was waiting for my driver and that if he didn't show up; I would walk up to the main road and catch a taxi. I thanked this man and the security guard and after another 15 minutes, it was time for me to find my own way back to the hotel. I wasn't sure where the driver was and as I hadn't paid him, I felt sure he was here somewhere as it would be unlikely he would have left without being paid. But I had another meeting and I couldn't wait anymore.

I thanked the security guard again and offered him a tip but he refused to take it. He had been very kind to me and I was grateful for all that he tried to do. Saying thank you didn't acknowledge how I felt and I remembered Ahmed's words "there are many people who will want to help you, but many of them have their own interests at heart". This man was definitely one who wanted to help and who had my interests at heart and I was grateful to him. I thought there really are a lot of great people in this world.

I took the elevator to the Ground Floor of the South Tower and walked out to the street. I must have looked quite a sight being the only woman here and a Western woman at that. I was looking everywhere for my driver, just in case he was still here somewhere. The security guards were watching me and so were the German Shepherds. As much as I love dogs and even used to have German Shepherds, now was not the time to say hello – these were working dogs after all. I couldn't see my driver anywhere and so I headed onto the main road.

The little black and white taxis are everywhere and it only took a second before one pulled up. I asked him how much to take me to the Ramses Hotel. He said 20 pound and I said no, 10 pound. He said 20 pound and I thought I can't be bothered arguing and said

13

OK. When I reflected on this later, I came to realize that I am a soft negotiator and have a tendency to give in easily.

I hopped in and soon discovered the state of the car. There was upholstery missing on the back seats, the car was started by hot wiring it and I found the contrast of this and say being in the Ambassador's office amusing. This is the real Egypt and this is the best way to understand life through their eyes. I completely enjoyed this experience, driving parallel to the Nile on a hot and beautiful sunny day with all the windows down catching the breeze to keep cool. I found a common theme in my travels was that of extremes – extreme wealth and extreme poverty. There were times when it was difficult for me to reconcile what I was seeing and feeling as it bought up many complex feelings for me to work through.

There were three lanes of traffic and we were in the fast lane. The car started to make some interesting noises and before long we were losing power. Wow I thought, the car is going to break down – this is the most interesting day I've had in a long time and I saw the humor in it and I started giggling. We coasted across the three lanes of traffic (I don't know how) and ended up on the side of the road. I knew we weren't far from the hotel and knew I could easily walk there if I had to. The only issue would be crossing the road. My driver said "one minute". He jumped out of the car, lifted the bonnet, did something, closed the bonnet and hopped back in. He started the car and it worked, we could now continue our journey.

To get to the hotel, we had to make a left hand turn across the traffic and as we did this, the car started to die again. He coasted it to the side of the road to let me out. I paid him the 20 pound which he was grateful for and I sensed his anguish over the condition of the car. I felt sorry for him and wondered what he would have to do to get the car fixed and how much it would cost. He certainly wasn't going to be earning any money as long as the car wasn't working.

Back on the hotel grounds, I needed to find the bellman. When I found him, he was very happy to see me. I explained to him what had happened; that the driver didn't pick me up at 12 'o'clock, how long I had waited for him, that I hadn't paid his driver and that I caught a taxi back. He didn't believe me asserting that the driver was still there. He pulled out his phone and made a few calls. Then he said "OK, I charge you 25 pound". And I said "no". I will pay you 20 pound and I looked him straight in the eye and with a firm voice said "you make sure the driver gets this money".

It turned out the driver was still in the car park, he had waited all this time and I was certain that he wouldn't get paid. It felt like the bellman controlled the power here and I felt a sense of anger creep up as the driver was in a powerless position and that didn't feel right for me. I felt sorry for him and it reminded me of the importance of being literate, being able to read and write and also about standing in your own power. When you cannot read, you give your power away and often power is mis-used and this was the dynamic that I felt with the driver and the bellman. I hoped I was wrong.

The morning had been a mini adventure and I needed a break. There was a little vendor selling coffee and cake on the ground floor of the hotel. Lunch today would be just that, coffee and a cake. The barista was a friendly man and although everything was served as a takeaway, I asked him where I could sit to have this. He pointed to some chairs not far away which is actually part of another restaurant so I took a spot there. The coffee was good, just what I needed. He kept watching me and after a few minutes, he came over to check to see if the coffee was OK. "It was perfect" I said, and he was happy.

After another meeting in the lobby, I returned to my room. Housekeeping had been in to tidy the room and to my surprise, they had made a collection of swans and ducks from the towels and left them on my bed and strategically placed around the room. It was totally awesome and a real gift. I thought wow - it's amazing what a tip can do. I now had face cloths, a multitude of towels and everything in the room had been replenished. Just as I thought this, there was a knock at the door.

"Housekeeping" again I wondered? Indeed it was Housekeeping and he had come back to take photos of the ducks and swans. He was very proud of his creations and it must have taken him quite some time to do all of this. He gave me a guided tour, explaining in detail which ones were the ducks, which ones were the swans and then of course, there were the baby ones. It was a nice surprise and a really

15

nice gesture and I thanked him. He was very happy when he left, like he was glad to be of service and to be appreciated for his efforts.

By now the traffic was at peak hour, busy and noisy. I went out to the balcony to survey the scene and felt glad that tomorrow I'd be leaving the chaos of Cairo for some space and some clean air.

Chapter 3

SHARM EL SHEIKH

Ahmed came early to take me to the airport for the flight to Sharm El Sheikh, which is on the Sinai peninsular of Egypt, not far from Israel and Jordan. The drive to the airport was as crazy as always. On some stretches of the road, there are two lanes marked and yet there are three, four or more lanes of traffic, as the cars create their own path here. It's like driving on a race track – you can pass on either side and that's where the tooting comes in, so the cars know you're coming through. You can easily put your hand out the window and touch the car next to you but the thing that really got me was the people trying to cross the road. There were at least two times that I had to close my eyes when we were doing 80km/hour and it looked like the people crossing the road were about to get hit by a car. Despite the chaos, apparently there are few accidents here. I wondered if maybe Egypt had the best drivers in the world.

My flight to Sharm El Sheikh went like clockwork. Arriving in Sharm El Sheikh was like arriving in paradise. From the air, I could see the contrast of the desert sands to the mountains and to the sea. There were palm trees and the most expensive looking houses, hotels and buildings I'd seen so far. The airport was brand new, extensive and glistened in the golden sun. I learnt that this is the most popular resort destination for Russian people to holiday and I sensed a lot of money changed hands here.

It was a full flight and my bag was the second one to come out. As I headed out of the airport, I started to look for my local guide. It was a hot 38 degrees Celsius outside and although there were lots of guides holding signs with clients' names on them, not one had my name on it. Hmmm, this is a bit unusual I thought, especially since the flight was late arriving. I stood in the sun and double checked every guide and their sign but to no avail.

I wondered what to do. I pulled out my itinerary and realized that the man standing next to me was a representative of the resort I was staying at. I asked him if he was meant to take me, or if he knew my representative, the latter which of course he did, but said he wasn't there. My name was not on his list and he was not interested in helping me. He turned away, to once again look for his passengers exiting the airport.

Another man approached me and I explained the dilemma showing him my itinerary. He could read English and rang the first contact number I had been given, only to discover that it was incorrect. He said he didn't have enough money on his phone to ring the mobile number that I had so he went away. But he came back a minute or so later and made the call for me anyway. He told me to go back inside the terminal and someone would meet me there. Meanwhile, another man came over and said he'd take me to the resort. He said he was the resort manager. I told him that I had been told to go back inside and wait. He said "no, come with me". I declined his offer and started walking towards the terminal when he called out "I will take you to the hotel and the bus will leave in five minutes".

I didn't want to miss the bus but I also didn't want to leave if someone was waiting for me. Fortunately when I got inside the terminal, there were two men waiting to help me and for some reason, they did not know I was arriving today so we agreed that catching the resort bus was the best thing to do. We raced out of the airport and ran to stop the bus which was just leaving.

As we drove to the resort, I realized I was staying in Sharm El Sheikh, whereas in my mind I thought I was staying at Dahab, which is about an hour away. I wondered why I was staying at a golf resort when I do not play golf.

The resort was stunning and it was rated five star and it was five star. If you like golf, then this is the perfect place to stay. It's also very family friendly with an amazing swimming pool that I know my daughter would love and you can easily snorkel in the Red Sea from a number of platforms that are built over the coral reef that are simply amazing. For me it was a culture shock coming from the hectic life of Cairo and the conservative dress, to the relaxed atmosphere of being at a resort by the sea, with everyone wandering around in swimwear.

Once I was checked in, I then made a few phone calls so that I would know what was happening for the next two days of my itinerary and the times for the pickups. I was told that a representative would meet me at the lobby at 5pm to apologize for today's mix up and to confirm the plan for the tomorrow. In the meantime, I had a couple of hours to fill so I thought I would enjoy some sunshine and laze by the pool.

Just after 4pm, I got back to my room when the phone rang. It was the local representative who was now waiting for me in the lobby. He thought we were to meet at 4pm and I'd been told it was 5pm. It was turning out to be one of those days.

I went to the lobby and met 'Awesome' who, with a big smile said it was the easiest way to remember his name in English. I laughed. He was right; it was the easiest way to remember his name.

Tomorrow, we would be visiting St Katherine's Monastery which is about 2.5 hours away. I explained to him how I had wanted to stay at Dahab and that my intent was to climb Mt Sinai but this was not on the itinerary. I realized it was my fault as I had not been specific enough with the original bookings. He said he might be able to organize it for me and I got my hopes up just long enough to come slamming down a minute later when he realized my return flight to Cairo wouldn't give us enough time. He was adamant that I would not like Dahab and that Sharm was a much nicer place to stay. He touched a nerve in me as I found myself thinking, how would he know what I would like when he doesn't even know me?

Unfortunately, this thought stayed with me for quite a while, that I realized there was something here that I needed to learn. Is it true that I know what is best for me and could it also be true that a complete stranger knows what's best for me too? Maybe I needed to be more open to other people's views and maybe a stranger sees in us that which we can't see in ourselves.

Either way, I was disappointed that I wasn't going to Mt Sinai. I had set my heart on being there and I had completely screwed up. My inner critic had a field day with this and I came to realize that my inner critic is worse than any other possible critic in the world. I chose to let go of these unhelpful thoughts and to think more empowering ones like, enjoy the moment, allow it to unfold and enjoy and be grateful for what you have. Our inner critic keeps us small and I had spent years worrying about what other people thought of me when I learnt a most valuable lesson here last year - what matters most is not what others think of me but what I think of myself.

I decided tomorrow it would be best for me to get back to my routine of getting up early, doing my yoga exercise and meditation, starting the day with peace and gratitude.

Chapter 4

ST KATHERINE'S MONASTERY

I had a sleepless night. I was worried that my alarm would not go off at 5am so I spent the night constantly waking up to check the time. It was 4.30 in the morning and I was wide awake so I got up. We would be driving for over five hours today and I definitely needed some exercise. I did my yoga practice finishing with a meditation. I felt great and I was ready for the day ahead.

The hotel advertised breakfast was available from 6am which was perfect for this early morning start. I was there at 6am but nothing was ready. In fact, there were no staff and there was no food. It was a rather slow process but I did manage to get a cup of tea and some pastries before I left half an hour later. I really wanted two fried eggs and I even contemplated cooking them myself. Then I said to myself, 'Jo, go with the flow. Maybe today you are not meant to have fried eggs' and besides, if I continued at this rate, I will have had twenty-eight eggs in two weeks!

The drive to Mt Sinai was amazing. I felt the sense of adventure and discovery before me and I was in my element, loving every minute of this. I had a wonderful driver, Haashim, who told me that he usually worked in Cairo but was here this week to help out a very busy local office and he loved talking English with me. 'Awesome' was in top form and I knew we'd all have a great day together.

This was the desert and despite the poverty in Egypt, I was impressed at how good the roads were. There were numerous military checkpoints to go through and I asked "Awesome" why this was so. He said it was because this was the main road to Israel and therefore the checks were part of border control.

The land is harsh and rugged and I found it difficult to imagine how people lived here but they do. They local people are Bedouin and you get glimpses of their remote villages from the road. The small houses are simple, built with bricks and mortar. People are poor here and we drove past children walking to a nearby school that the Government had built for them. Some children have to walk for three or four kilometers to get there, yet it is a great thing that these kids are getting an education in such a remote place.

The landscape changed as we increased our altitude. Basically, being in the desert everything was sand or rock, with the odd acacia tree for greenery. When it rains here, there are great floods and this is evident by the flood plains and the way the road is built. With such sheer mountains all around and lots of loose rock, it must be quite a sight to see when the rains come.

We were the only car on the road when 'Awesome' told Haashim to stop and he got out. Haashim and I had no idea what he was doing but we knew that he was up to something and we both began to laugh. He came back with some plants. In the valleys, wild chamomile grows here and I learnt that this keeps the snakes and scorpions away. There was also another plant that grows wild here and we stopped a bit further on where 'Awesome' picked some from the side of the road. I have forgotten the name of it, but it was a green round fruit and he showed me how to use it medicinally to treat arthritis.

Then out of the blue, 'Awesome' said he had a surprise for me. He said he could arrange a Bedouin guide to meet with me and take me a small way up Mt Sinai but if I wanted to do this, then we wouldn't have time to see Dahab as well. I pondered on my choices and with a big smile, I told him that I wanted to do both, but mostly I wanted to do Mt Sinai. He started to make some calls and within minutes, it had been arranged. 'Awesome' turned out to be awesome and I was rapt.

The colors changed from the golden/white sand to green, yellow, red and black due to the minerals in the earth. The mountains themselves are simply beautiful and I felt sure that many centuries ago, most of what we were driving on was underwater. Some of the mountains and rocks reminded me of the Pancake Rocks in New Zealand.

Arriving at St Katherine's Monastery, 'Awesome' negotiated a camel ride for me for 10 pound. I turned it down but thought this was something that I must do while I am in Egypt. The monastery is run by 15 monks who follow the Greek Orthodox Church, which reminded me of my time in Greece earlier in the year. In fact, coming here is a bit like being in Greece as the area is planted with olive trees and herbs like rosemary. It was not what I expected to see in Egypt.

The monastery was named after St Katherine, who was a legendary martyr from Alexandria and a proponent of the Christian religion. She was tortured and be-headed for her faith. It is believed that her body was transported by angels to a mountain not far from Mt Sinai where her body was found there, some 300 years later perfectly preserved.

The monastery is one of the oldest functioning monasteries in the world and many have made their pilgrimage here in what would have been a difficult journey as the site is so remote. The place I loved the most was the burning bush where it is believed that God spoke to Moses. The museum here is also fantastic, with plenty of well-preserved ancient books and art.

As we left St Katherine's, we walked down the road when 'Awesome' saw a reddish stone in the sand. He picked it up and gave it to me. I asked him what it was and he said "it's a holy stone from here, take it with you". He handed it to me and despite the odd shape, it fitted perfectly in the palm of my hand. It felt special.

Next we drove for about five minutes to pick up my Bedouin guide Mohamed, who would walk me part of the way towards Mt Sinai. Mohamed was a lean man, with a wonderful smile and a very gentle manner. I liked him immediately and knew intuitively, he was the right man to guide me.

The trek to the top of Mt Sinai is generally done before sunrise or in the late afternoon before sunset. It takes 3 to 4 hours and contains 750 steps towards the top which are the hardest part. We turned off the main road and the road became a bumpy dirt track which would have been much easier in a four wheel drive vehicle. We drove very slowly for over 15 minutes passing tiny Bedouin villages. I was mesmerized by what I saw and totally loving this moment. I loved the simplicity of life here.

We were off the beaten track and in a very remote area. I had no idea where we were when a thought popped into my head – am I safe? Here I am in a vehicle with 3 men I do not know, I don't speak the language, nor do I know where I am. I dismissed this thought. I just knew I was meant to be here and that's all I needed to know. We stopped at a large village and Mohamed told me to follow him. Jokingly, I checked with 'Awesome' that he would still be there when I got back. He said "of course".

We walked uphill for about 15 minutes through rough and loose rock in the searing heat of midday and I wondered how far we had to go. When I lost my footing Mohamed offered me his hand and waited for me to catch up. He made it look so easy. He led me to this amazing rock in the shade with the most magnificent views of Mt Sinai. We didn't have much time so I asked him if I could meditate. He sat silently next to me, patiently waiting as I closed my eyes and went into a deep meditative space.

The energy was very pure and strong here and I immediately felt it through my body. It was so quiet and there was no noise. I felt a deep level of peace wash over me and I knew I had been here before. As I opened my eyes, Mohamed checked to see if I was OK and then offered to take my photo, showing me the best place to stand. This was a moving experience and I felt a deep sense of gratitude for the opportunity, literally off the beaten track and so unique. I realized the inherent wisdom that I was not meant to walk up Mt Sinai on this trip. There is a spiritual saying that 'everything is in Divine and perfect order' and indeed it is.

Mohamed told me that he climbs Mt Sinai twice a day and about 600 people make the trek, although many do not have the fitness to get to the top. It was no wonder that he looked so lean and so fit. I imagined him gliding up there making it look so easy and effortless and he reminded me of the importance of taking care of our physical bodies through the food we eat, exercise and physical fitness.

We headed back down to the vehicle and I was intrigued by the local village that we walked passed. There was something magic about the people here and I would have loved to have had a cup of tea with them and to understand life through their eyes. The houses are basic, built of bricks, mortar and local wood. The most common vehicle here is a Toyota Hilux which is perfect for the conditions.

That half an hour was like gold to me, so precious, unique and peaceful. It was imprinted in my mind and heart.

We drove back to St Katherine's to drop Mohamed off and then stopped for lunch. It was hot now and I was glad of some shade and water. We chatted over lunch and I saw another side to 'Awesome' when he told me that his wife was seriously injured in a car crash a few months ago. She was hospitalized in Cairo, was paralyzed and their four children were staying amongst their families in Cairo too. His wife needed daily medical care and he was hoping that they would all return home in November. It had been a hard time for them all and my heart went out to them.

After lunch we headed back and 'Awesome' showed me precisely where the accident occurred. It sent a chill through my spine. Then, he told me there was enough time to visit Dahab which was another place I wanted to go to. Again, I thought 'Awesome', you really are awesome. Thank you.

The drive back seemed completely different to the drive there. As if 'Awesome' read my mind, he said the exact same thing. This time when I looked at the mountains, they became alive. I saw faces, cities and pyramids and knew intuitively that there was much ancient wisdom stored here.

Along the way, we talked about all sorts of things, like how he came to be in this line of work; integrity and the lack of it in business and why all the men here smoke. 'Awesome' explained that smoking was all about being a man and that you were teased if you didn't smoke because you're not considered a man; you were a Mummy's boy, Haashim started laughing and nodding his head in agreement. I understood completely and it reminded me that as women, we need to nurture the spirit of the men in our lives and let them be men.

Dahab is a seaside resort town with lots of shopping along a wonderful esplanade on the waterfront of the Red Sea. As we wandered along, we noticed air bubbles in the sea. 'Awesome' said that the drop off was very deep here and that surprisingly, you could dive in as little as 50m from the shore.

I peered over the walkway and found a beautiful young girl making something; necklaces, bookmarks, I wasn't sure what they were, but she offered one to me and I shook my head to say no. Then, I noticed she was making them with her feet. With her eyes, a glowing smile and a gesture of her hand, she asked me again and I shook my head. Then when I looked into her eyes once more, I saw such a beautiful gentle child and I wondered what had happened to her in her lifetime. She looked disabled and it felt like she had been placed there for the day, as if she had been abandoned and it reminded me of my own inner child that once had been abandoned too. I would have loved to have sat and stayed with her but 'Awesome' kept walking and ushered me on.

I was becoming aware that people who go to the effort to make something or do something in order to make a living, were the people I wanted to support, rather than those who just ask for money because you are a tourist. Later, when I reflected on this little girl and thought about my own daughter, I realized how easy it is for her to be given money for doing nothing, and yet these children were already entrepreneurs, running their own small business to help their families. I really wished I had given her something and made her day.

We drove back to Sharm El Sheikh and we passed the school once again. I wondered what teaching resources they had and what they needed. I thought what fun it would be to have a huge canvas and to paint a mural with them.

By the time we got back to the hotel, I realized that 'Awesome' was totally awesome – he was so knowledgeable and so well connected. He was one of the best tour guides I have had and it was easy to see why he got a lot of repeat business and clients asking for him by name. He knew everyone and he knew how to make things happen. I had the most amazing day, thanks to him and Haashim too.

I was back at the hotel by 4pm which gave me enough time to snorkel the Red Sea before the sun went down around five and darkness arrived not long after. I thanked them both for the awesome day and raced to my room to get changed.

Swimming in the Red Sea was another amazing experience. The water was so clear, the fish so colorful and the coral amazing. I felt exhilarated with a sense of euphoria at being given this opportunity. The waters were a warm 27 degrees Celsius (ironically the swimming pool was 26 degrees Celsius) and I was in heaven. What a perfect finish to a perfect day.

This was another one of those surreal moments when I felt so grateful, that I wondered how on earth I ended up here and it was the second time today that I had felt this way.

I loved it here and wished there was more time to explore and continue up to Jordan and even Israel but I know that's for another time. For now, I needed to go back to Cairo, then on to the Western Desert next week.

Chapter 5

BACK TO CAIRO

I had totally adjusted to Sharm El Sheikh but I knew it was like living in a bubble. Today I had breakfast and the chef cooked me two fried eggs. As he went to flip one over, the yoke broke, he looked at me and I said it was OK. This wasn't good enough for him so he scraped it into the rubbish bin. Truly, that was a waste.

I thought of the little girl I saw on the beach at Dahab yesterday and wondered what she would be having for breakfast, or would she be having breakfast at all? The lyrics of Phil Collin's song "it's just another day in paradise" ran through my mind. As I sipped my tea, the more I thought about her, the more the tears filled my eyes. How is it I can be sitting here in this beautiful resort with such an extensive buffet and yet a few kilometers away, people are living in poverty? I grappled with the lack of equality – today, it just didn't feel right. As I looked around me, everyone here was on holiday and it seemed like no-one cared about what they couldn't see or chose not to see which is the other side of life in Egypt. Yet, everyone wants a better quality of life for their families and for themselves. I wondered how do we work together to make this so?

I thought about the staff that worked here and tried to imagine how they lived, what their life was like and how much they were paid. Money flowed through this resort yet I suspected that not much of it flowed to those working at the front line.

William Wilberforce who pioneered the abolition of slavery said so powerfully in the movie Amazing Grace, "that God created us equal". He is my inspiration that not only can one person make a difference but that we all can. I know that being in poverty makes it hard to help others in poverty and I was looking forward to expanding my knowledge through reading the books I had bought in Singapore by the well known professors C.K Prahalad "The Fortune at the Bottom of the Pyramid – Eradicating Poverty through Profits" and Philip Kotler's "Up and Out of Poverty".

After breakfast, I checked out and met up with a new driver called Musad and a local guide Hazir to take me to the airport. Hazir said "remember me; I met you at the airport the other day?" Initially I didn't remember him as there were so many people I met that day but then he came back to me. He remembered how heavy my suitcase was and that I had explained to him that my suitcase was full of children's clothing and art supplies to give to the children in a village in Giza.

Sharm El Sheikh is home to many Middle Eastern conferences that discuss the issues of the region and there is a large billboard that has the photos of many of our world leaders on it with the slogan 'peace'. This is where the peace talks happen and as such, it is surrounded by military guards everywhere. For me, I had certainly found a deep inner peace here that I had not felt before and I was grateful for my brief time here.

On the way to the airport, Hazir and I talked about my trip yesterday. Hazir told me how lucky I was to have 'Awesome'. He said he was the best guide here and he knows everyone. It was wonderful to hear someone talking about a fellow staff member with such high regard that it reminded me of my corporate days and the need to do just that – to support and talk up your colleagues and recognize them for their inherent strengths.

Hazir was amazing at the airport. There were three counters open for check in and we lined up in what looked like the shortest one. The airline staff were checking in another passenger, when

Hazir took my passport and ticket and started talking with him. Whatever he said, it didn't work and I could see the answer was a clear 'no'. He told me to stay here and went over to another queue and started talking with the staff member there. In a flash, my suitcase was checked in, I was upgraded to business class and given a complimentary voucher for a tea or coffee at the cafe. Wow, I thought, that was impressive. Sometimes it is true, that it's who you know that makes the difference but I was also curious to know what he had said too!

Patience is required when traveling with Egypt Air as I had yet to experience a flight leaving on time. At the departure gate, I knew I had time on my side so I pulled out my computer and continued writing about my journey here. I came to realize that something significant in me had shifted and knew that it occurred at Mt Sinai. I had been here less than forty-eight hours and yet, I felt very alive, refreshed and a profound sense of inner peace. Sharm had been good for my soul.

Once on the plane, I was offered an English newspaper. I hadn't heard or seen any news for days and actually I prefer it this way as so much of what is reported keeps us in fear. There was one article that caught my eye. It was the one about the upcoming elections in Egypt. An international group had stated that there was corruption in the election process and they were lobbying for the election to be overseen and run by an independent international group following international protocols. I wondered if this would happen or was the system here so corrupt that those in power would undermine this group and they would be silenced. And then I thought about the role of Government and how it is there, in theory to serve all the people and the environment. From what I could see, the needs of the vast majority of people here are not met and I wondered how prosperous life would be if there was no corruption.

We landed in Cairo. A VIP, who was in Business Class, was whisked away to his private entourage awaiting him with a car on the tarmac. I had no idea who this person was and like everyone else, I was curious to know. The rest of us were transported to the terminal by bus. I chuckled to myself when my bag arrived before the VIPs and as a result, I was the first one out.

Now, who was picking me up today? I couldn't see my name anywhere and I couldn't see anyone I knew. I stopped to consider what to do next, wondering if there had been another mix up, when out of nowhere came Ahmed. I realized how nice it was to see a familiar face and how grateful I was to have Ahmed, who was always smiling, enthusiastic and full of energy. He led me to the car and was very interested to know everything that had happened to me in the last two days.

I met Hossam who was our driver today. We were back in very busy Cairo traffic and Hossam was a genius at getting us through the maze of cars, literally an inch on either side of us. Hossam's driving ability was truly impressive and I was glad to learn that he would be my driver into the Desert alongside Ahmed.

Cairo is such a contrast to Sharm, but I was in such a good space that somehow I was ready to be back here again.

Chapter 6

GIZA

I had chosen to stay in a hotel as close as you could get to the Pyramids. This was a real treat. Like most things, I am sure if you see them every day, you begin to take them for granted. This area of town called Giza is naturally busy and full of tourists with most people dressed in typical western style - shorts, t-shirts, dresses and skirts.

After I had checked in, I rang my New Zealand friend, Rosemary who lives here to tell her that I had arrived. Rosemary said she would come and pick me up about 7pm and take me to her house - a short five minute drive away. I was loaded with bags full of children's clothes, coloring books, felt tip pens and coloring pencils to give to the children of her village. Ahmad, her Egyptian husband, would help us to make sure the right items went to those most in need.

We spent the night talking and catching up. We shared some Egyptian takeaways delivered by motorbike and I met many local people who stopped by. Outside, loud music filled the streets as a wedding was in progress with much celebration. Life felt busy here.

It was after midnight when we realized the time. Rosemary walked me to the main road to catch a taxi back to the hotel. It was very busy and lots of people were hanging around, mostly men, who stared at me. I started to feel self-conscious and vulnerable.

Rosemary said that taxis pass here all the time and it wouldn't take long to flag one down. But it took longer than we thought. Meanwhile a group of three men had crossed the road and while I was looking the other way, they came right up beside me and said "Hi beautiful, what's your name". I got such a fright that I literally jumped and ended up on the opposite side of Rosemary. I realized how afraid I was. I asked her if it was safe here and she said, "to trust" and "watch my thoughts". I was feeling afraid and I had created this situation so I silently asked Archangel Michael, the great protector to stand with me while we waited.

A taxi pulled over and Rosemary spoke in Arabic to the driver. He assured us he knew where the hotel was but again, I was afraid that he didn't know where to go. What should have been a five minute drive took about twenty five minutes. He took me to a hotel, but it wasn't the one I was staying at and I didn't know where it was either. He stopped to ask someone on the side of the road and we repeated the same circuit, ending up at the wrong hotel again. He tried again, stopping to ask two different people and by now, I was feeling incredibly fearful. I started to think about what to do and in my mind I made a plan. I knew that my hotel could not be far from where he had taken me and I thought if we ended up there again, I'd get out and ask the hotel staff for help. Just then, he found it. I was relieved and it was a great lesson to me on how our thoughts create our reality.

By now, my nerves were a bit frazzled that I found it hard to sleep. When I finally did get some sleep, I awoke to a horrendous screeching of tyres and a car crash outside the hotel that even woke the people in the room next to me. I hoped no-one was injured and with what seemed like an eternity, I eventually heard the car start again and drive off.

I discovered the next day that my hotel was literally on the opposite corner from where the taxi driver had taken me last night. I now had my bearings and knew where I was and that gave me a great sense of confidence.

I went back to Rosemary's house the next day and we thought carefully about the best way to give out the clothes and art materials that I had bought with me. We ended up grouping three items of clothing into age bands and then placed them in separate bags. These would be given to children and families with the greatest need. Typically these were families where there was no husband or father present.

In Egypt, women typically work until they are married. After that, their role is to manage the house and they rely on the men in the family to provide for them. So, without a husband or a father, women rely on their brothers for support and families struggle to buy the bare necessities like food. Clothing is generally borrowed from others and Ahmad knew exactly who was in most need and knew who to give what items to. We had another bag of hats and pens that we gave out more freely.

We decided that the art materials, felt tip pens, crayons, coloring pencils and books were too difficult to hand out and would create more problems than it solved. I had planned to visit an orphanage while in Luxor and we agreed it would be best to take them there, as they had the structure in place to ensure they would get to where they were needed most and they also had a pre-school. Luxor was the end part of my journey so these items traveled with me all through Egypt and the desert!

The village was a maze of connected houses built on sand about three stories high. Some of the alleyways are just wide enough to fit a car through and of course, they are shared with the donkey and cart, horses, motorbikes, people and children playing. Then there are a multitude of very small businesses each being about the size of a small room that act as the local shops like a dairy, a dry-cleaner, a barber, a restaurant and food shops although fresh produce is usually sold off the donkey cart.

It was like a mini city, a hub of activity of different noises, like the regular call for prayer at the mosques and of course, the vast range of smells from food cooking to the fresh horse dung. I wanted to see inside the typical house which I knew was very basic, yet there is something magical about the simplicity of life here. It helped me to understand and appreciate more fully the micro-financing loans that we had started through Great Spirit New Zealand www.greatspirit.co.nz and Kiva www.kiva.org.

Walking though the village was an experience in itself. It would not be common for a Western woman to be seen in the village. I felt many eyes following me and guessed people were wondering who I was and why I was here. And why were we carrying all these plastic bags and more importantly, what were inside them? It gave me great insight into everyday Egyptian life.

The first child we gave a bag to was a young boy that was about six years old. The smile on his face was electric. You could see in his eyes that he couldn't believe his luck as we showed him the clothes making sure they would fit him. His excitement was contagious; the joy of an unexpected gift and all new clothes. He ran off at speed, with glee and joy in his stride – it really was a beautiful sight to see.

In another family, we gave about three bags of clothing to the mother, who had a number of children and a husband in prison. As we spoke in Arabic, I looked past her noticing that they were cooking dinner with a very small gas cooker – about the size for one small pot. There wasn't much furniture or anything here; it was the basic necessities of life. We gave all the children pens and the mother was genuinely very grateful. She offered her hand to me, then looked me straight in the eye to say thank you in English. There was a hint of tears in her eyes and I could tell that life was not easy for her at all. Being a mother too, I felt her pain and I felt the love in her heart. It was another moving experience.

We continued around the village and before long we had a lot of mothers and children following us, a bit like the 'Pied Piper". At one stage, it got chaotic as everyone wanted something and Ahmad was great at managing the demands, although it was difficult for him to say 'no' too. We noticed that those with the loudest voice or who pushed in the most were never the ones in real need. Those in real need never asked. They stood back and were quiet. Another thing we noticed was that if the clothes were too big or small, the mothers wouldn't take them just for the sake of having something.

One image that I will never forget is the little two year old boy who so desperately wanted the white hat that had ears. At this stage, we were surrounded by a large group of mothers and children. Now the hat was too small for him and he had been told this a couple of times. He had even tried it on and he knew it didn't fit. He was determined and with that determination, he got his way and grabbed the hat. He was so proud of himself and had the biggest grin you could imagine. He ran off down the alley clutching his hat, filled with joy and shouting at anyone who was there. I imagine he was saying "look what I've got". It was a magical moment and we just hoped he wouldn't fall over and land in the mud!

This was a humbling experience and a great reminder to me that most of us have far more than we really need. Just by being grateful for what we have is far more important and fulfilling than the belief that we always need more.

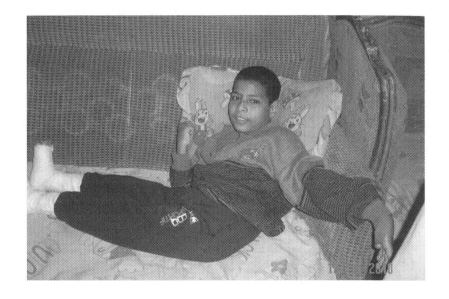

19 2 2010

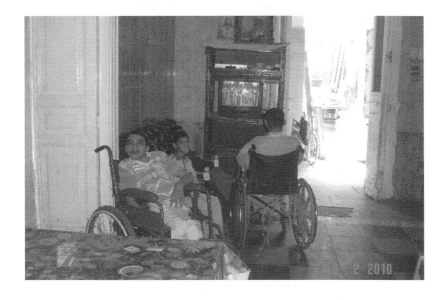

Chapter 7

THE PYRAMIDS

I was excited to be visiting the Pyramids today. I wanted to go inside to the King's Chamber of the pyramid known as Cheops. Each day the ticket office limits the number of people who can go inside and as such, there are only two times to get tickets – either 8am or 1pm. I was planning for the 1pm session and thought I'd have an hour or two by the pool while I waited.

To get to the Pyramids, I had the choice to hail a taxi from the main road or to use the hotel taxi. Against better judgment, I asked the man at the hotel desk for the price to take me to the Pyramids. We started negotiating, as I felt the amount was too much and I was now getting much wiser to the pricing here. All I needed was someone to get me to the entrance. We debated a little more and I clearly explained what I wanted to do and they were adamant it was not wise for me to go there alone and that I needed a guide, neither of which I agreed with. I am not quite sure what happened next as there was an exchange in Arabic; I thought they had understood what I wanted and I had understood the price.

I met Atif, who would be my driver and we walked to the car. Having been at Rosemary's house, I now knew my way around and we drove for a few minutes when I began to realize I was being taken to the Sphinx end of Giza, and not the main entrance to the

Pyramids. When I asked where we were going, he said he was taking me to get a camel ride. I hadn't agreed to a camel ride but I decided that it was OK as it was one of the things I had wanted to do while in Egypt.

Time was of the essence as it was already 1.30pm and I wanted to get the ticket to enter the King's Chamber. I was introduced to the owner of the camels who told me an all-encompassing camel trip would be 360 Egyptian pounds. This wasn't what I wanted and I told him so and then turned to Atif for help. In a firm voice, I said that all I wanted to do was to visit the King's Chamber and the Sphinx and he told me the "truth" that it would be too late for me to get a ticket to the King's Chamber. I said "but that's why I came here" and he said "I'm sorry" but you may have to come back in the morning. And that's how I ended up on a camel ride. Ahmed's words once again rang true and I had not discerned the truth that this man was lying to me and I had in fact, allowed myself to be set up once again.

In a flash, I was on the camel – it was not a great choice to have worn a skirt, but then I was not expecting to be riding a camel today. As the camel got up, I nearly fell off. It was a good thing that they all yelled at me to hold on tight. The Egyptians make it look so easy and riding horses was never my thing, so a camel....well it's just a bit higher off the ground. Quietly, I spoke to the camel's soul, letting him know that I meant him no harm, that I had come in peace, with love and that I was grateful for the ride.

A young boy called Abdul led my camel and Mohammad my guide rode beside me on his horse. As we walked down the road, out of nowhere came a man on another horse who pulled up beside me and who then offered me an Egyptian headscarf. I naively thought it was part of the tour. After he had put it on my head and explained how to wear it, he asked for 30 pounds. I looked at him in disbelief, now realizing my error, and said that it was too much. We ended up on 20 pounds, not that I needed it and I know I had paid too much but I justified it to myself by saying it was hot, I needed some shade plus I thought Hannah my daughter would enjoy it when I got home. My guide Mohammad reminded me that he had already told me that many people would approach me in the street selling stuff and not to buy anything. I said, "why didn't you remind me?" He said "it wouldn't be right". By now, I had realized I'd been taken for a ride in the literal sense and decided that I was here now and that I would make the most of it.

We entered the Giza site from the desert and had the most magnificent views of six of the nine pyramids, of Saqqara, an area I love plus great views of Cairo city. Going uphill on the camel was fine, going downhill, well that's an experience! Mohammad had to yell at me to lean back, which became a delicate balance between doing that and still being able to hold on.

Mohammad loved the actor Jim Carrey so every five minutes or so, he would say "don't worry, be happy, and remember me I am Jim Carrey". And then laugh. And I laughed too. He spoke great English and I found out that he came from Alexandria, a city north of Cairo. He was studying languages and typical of most Egyptian men, he first asked my age and then if I was married.

Abdul who walked the camel was about nine years old and he smiled at me the whole time. I asked if he went to school and he did, but he was on holiday because the Government had closed a number of schools due to the swine flu. Together they taught me a few Egyptian words subsequently forgotten but essentially how to make the camel go faster! Mohammad was adamant that after riding the camel I would be "walking like an Egyptian"...you know the song followed by more of his laughter.

They took me in the direction of the ticket booth and it was well after 2pm when we got there. I raced over delighted to find that tickets were still available for the King's Chamber. The attendant told me to hurry as they would close it off in about ten minutes. So that's what I did.

I climbed the stairs to the entrance and I was thrilled to have finally made it. On the way up, lots of people were coming out and by the time I got into the King's Chamber, there were just three people there, all of whom left as I arrived. Here I was on my own, how unbelievably good was that!

I was sweating profusely and breathing hard from the steep incline into the Chamber. I focused on slowing my breathing and heart rate down so I could meditate. I am not sure how long I was in there, another man was there too but I closed my eyes, stood with my hands on the sarcophagus and went into a meditative space. I felt the sweat pouring out of me and my feet burning, the energy here pouring through my body. It was hard to quieten my mind, yet I knew it was not time to leave just yet. So I stayed until I knew intuitively, that it was time to go. When I left, the man was still there and then I realized he was one of the guards. Often, they will usher you to leave when they feel you have had enough time there. I knew it was divinely ordered that indeed I was meant to be there on my own. The energy was incredibly powerful and I knew that whatever had happened in here, I would feel the energetic shift in a few days' time.

When I left the King's Chamber, I felt complete, that I had done what I came here to do. I bought a bottle of water and then walked with Mohammad to the Sphinx. It was impressive but it didn't have the hold on me like it did last year. I came to understand that I was not the same person who was here a year ago, that so much in me had changed and therefore what I'd be attracted to would be different. What did intrigue me was an area not far from the Sphinx that had recently been uncovered. There were a number of tombs and Mohammad said I could visit and meditate there as long as we paid the guard. Sadly, I didn't have enough money on me to do that.

As we walked back to town (by now I had decided that walking was easier than camel riding so we had sent Abdul back with the camel), Mohammad saw my empty water bottle and told me to throw it on the ground. There are hundreds of plastic bottles strewn through the sand here and lots of rubbish too. I told him that I couldn't do that because I cared about the environment. He understood and agreed with me, but he said "everyone does it here".

He then caught me by surprise when he then asked me to pay him. I said that I would pay the owner who I had agreed the price with. He said the price didn't include him and I said as far as I was concerned it did. He smiled and tried again saying it would be best for me to pay him now and not at the office. Of course, we got to the office, I paid the owner and then they both told me that it didn't include Mohammad. Mohammad smiled and said that I didn't need to pay him if I didn't want to but this didn't feel right either so I gave him the only money I had left, a 20 pound note. Now, I was well and truly out of money and had paid the price for an important lesson around discernment.

The owner of the camels had a perfumery shop and Atif and I sat and talked while we waited for some tea. He was very interested in my work and what we had gifted to the children here. He listened intently to my words and when I spoke about helping children, he said "I can see the tears in your eyes; you have a very open heart and you have a real love of the people here". I told him about my spiritual tours and that I knew that I had many past lives here. Egypt is in my blood, it's in my heart and it's my spiritual home. He said, "there's someone I want you to meet and I will take you there now". "He is a healer like you".

And so we were off again on another adventure. Atif couldn't pronounce my name properly and so he called me Joy. He kept asking me why I wasn't married and I jokingly told him that there were no decent New Zealand men!

I wondered where we were going now. Within minutes, we pulled up to a healing center and I was introduced to the owner, Rasul. They make their own aromatherapy oils and Egyptian perfumes here and so it had the most glorious smell. The raw ingredients were stored in baskets and they showed me the machine they use to make the oil by hand. There were rows and rows of bottles of perfumes and I could have spent hours in here and probably spend a small fortune. After a quick tour, I was offered some tea and a chat. They brought me their brochure to read and I discovered they did spiritual tours to the desert too. I told him about my tours and we talked some more.

I noticed that Rasul had begun reading my energy and he said I had a very busy mind. I smiled and he asked one of his staff to bring the Lotus flower perfume out and said this would help. He then brought another perfume which had frankincense as the base oil and smelt divine. He said this would be great on my 3rd eye which is the center of the forehead.

Rasul asked me what I knew of my past lives in Egypt so I shared with him my knowledge. He agreed that I had been a High Priest and a ruler here. He said "you are a leader and leadership is your destiny in this lifetime. You have a very strong aura and your tours will be very successful". It was another one of those moments when I wondered how I ended up here, yet knowing it was divinely ordered and that I was meant to be here.

I didn't buy anything as I had run out of money. I thanked Rasul for the tour and tea and said goodbye. It was time to head back to the hotel. There was some Arabic exchanged between Atif and Rasul and I wondered what would come of this meeting.

Back at the hotel, I started to pack everything up as I'd be leaving for Siwa in the morning.

The safety deposit box was mounted high up in the wardrobe and I needed a chair to stand on so I could be sure that I had taken everything out. As I stood up on the chair, I forgot that the safety deposit door was open and I whacked my head into the sharp metal corner of the door. Quickly, I placed my hand over where it hurt and hoped that it was just a bang and not a major cut. The pain was intense and when I had the courage to take my hand away, the blood was pouring out. I quickly ran to the bathroom and grabbed a bunch of tissues and then thought I needed to find the Arnica (a homeopathic remedy).

At the same time, the phone rang and it was Ahmed. As if he knew, he asked me if everything was all right and it wasn't, but I said yes, not wanting to alarm him about the blood pouring out of my head. I was hoping I would be fine by tomorrow as I had no intention of visiting an Egyptian hospital. He confirmed that we would be leaving at 8am. I found the Arnica and the bleeding stopped. Now I just had a sore head and a rather large lump, fortunately just covered by my hair. And that was the end of yet another truly memorable day in Egypt!

Chapter 8

SIWA

We left Cairo at 8.30 in the morning in peak hour traffic and Ahmed told me it would take a long time to get to Siwa. We had about 800kms to drive and he thought we would arrive about 9pm.

The drive itself was quite incredible. Everywhere you look is desert and everything is built on sand. The roads are incredibly straight and flat, quite the opposite of driving around New Zealand. We would drive for ages and then out of nowhere would appear a city, really in the middle of nowhere.

We passed Alamein and I noticed the large German Memorial Site that is built there. And then I recalled that there were many New Zealanders that fought in this area. The NZ Ambassador told me that there were thousands of soldiers here at one time and so of course; this area is steeped in history with many who lost their lives as a consequence.

After a couple of hours of driving, we stopped at a busy tourist café with a bakery. I had a coffee while Hossam and Ahmed bought bread. I soon discovered that this was breakfast for them.

Back on the road again, it was funny to see a sign that advertised a McDonald's drive through. I thought this was a good idea as there was nothing for miles but as we drove past, it was closed. Like so many buildings I saw, they were empty. And yet there were signs advertising seaside resorts but again, these were either under construction or completely abandoned too.

Hossam, who was of Nubian descent, had brought some music for the long drive. I was introduced to his Nubian music which even Ahmed said he hadn't heard before either, as well as two beautiful women singers Elissa and Shirin. The music was great, easy to listen to and very much from the heart. Hossam and Ahmed turned out to be a great combination. They worked well together and I was glad to be traveling with them. They laughed and joked with each other, they shared their pistachios with me and sometimes they forgot I was even there and sometimes, I forgot they were there too!

We arrived in the city Matrouh which is the last major city before Siwa. It was about 3pm and Ahmed took me to a restaurant for lunch. It looked like it was closed and I think it was but it was suddenly opened for me. Ahmed said he and Hossam had a few things to do and they would come back for me soon. Meanwhile, I was the only person there and as much as the food was very nice, I would have preferred to have eaten with them. That is, if they actually had stopped to eat which I had a sneaky feeling they hadn't.

Back on the road, it was only 300kms to go now and we made good time. The desert sprawls for miles and miles. It's completely vast and flat with the odd bit of greenery from time to time. It was windy and things would move across the desert floor with speed as there was nothing to stop them. I loved seeing groups of wild camels and in many ways; they looked in better health than the ones I had seen in the cities. The roads really are so good and it was fun watching the sun go down and then driving by night.

We arrived in Siwa just before 8pm and because it was pitch black, it was hard to get a general feel to the place. Ahmed told me this was his first time here too but Hossam had been here before and knew exactly where we were going, which was great because there were no street signs or lights.

The hotel was extensive with many rooms, generally grouped in separate buildings of four. The walk to my room was like a maze and I hoped I'd remember how to find my way to the restaurant. The room was quite basic decorated with Egyptian rugs on the walls yet it was incredibly clean and tidy. The porter showed me how to turn on the TV but there seemed to be only one volume, which was very loud so I asked him to switch it off. There was a rather old style air-conditioning unit and as it was incredibly hot in the room, he switched it on which was great except for the noise which was unbearable (when I switched it off later, the control button actually came off in my hand!).

I imagined this would be rated here as a three star hotel and was another contrast to my hotel in Sharm El Sheikh. Travel and adjusting to change go hand in hand. I had come to learn that one of my greatest strengths was adaptability. I don't really mind where I stay as long as it is clean, has a toilet and a shower (preferably with hot water which is probably more than what most Egyptian homes have). I commonly found in Egypt that the hand basins had no plugs and it was not common to get face cloths either. This room was the same.

It was after 10pm by the time I made it to bed. I felt tired and hadn't realized how tired I was from the traveling. I knew I was in for a hot night, a night when you would wake up constantly dripping in sweat. No sooner had my head hit the pillow that I discovered a mosquito in the room. Now, this really frustrated me. I got back up and put mosquito repellent all over my arms and legs, found some lavender oil and put a few drops on my pillow and asked it to go away. I was still recovering from my last set of mosquito bites from the pool at Giza and this reminded me to remember to bring a small room spray next time. Then I drifted off to sleep oblivious to the mosquito.

It was very quiet and still here at night. The slightest noise was easily heard. I got a fright when I woke up to a man banging on the door shouting "this is your wake-up call". Although it sounded like my door, it was the room next to mine and he wouldn't leave until the guests had confirmed with him that they were indeed awake. Then he continued his rounds. Wow, I thought this was quite cool, the human touch - so much nicer than waking up to the buzzer of an alarm clock. I switched on the light, it was 6am.

By 10am, we were off to explore Siwa. The first stop was the Mountain of the Dead where it is believed there are over three hundred burial sites which resembled a honeycomb pattern. We visited a variety of underground tombs and as always, it was amazing to see the art on the walls depicting the story of what happened all those thousands of years ago. Ahmed and I climbed to the top of the mountain. The views were stunning, encompassing all of Siwa, to the lakes, the mountains, the villages and to the abundance of trees which looked like a great big green belt surrounding the township. I took a few minutes to do a short meditation blessing the land and honoring all those who were buried here and Ahmed offered to take my photo for me.

Then we drove to the 13th century fortress of Shali which is at the center of the town and high up on a hill. The buildings were made of salt, rock and plastered with clay. Most of the site had disintegrated with the rain, yet it was still impressive. It had spectacular views in all directions too and it would have been very effective as a fortress in its time. It was believed to be home to more than 300 families and at the lower levels, people still live there today.

On the way up, two children were watching me from the window of their house and called out 'hello". They were very cute and I realized that it would have made a fabulous photo.

The air was very clean here and the gentle breeze took away the heat of the day. It was peaceful and I found I could easily have stayed here for a while. On the way down, a little boy dressed in a bright yellow shirt ran out of his house, said hello and pointed to the items on the base of the stairs saying "this is my shop, would I like something"? I loved his entrepreneurial spirit. Sometimes I would find myself just wanting to give them some money as a reward for the effort they had made.

Next we visited the Temple of the Oracle where Alexander the Great sought advice in the 26th Dynasty. This temple was dedicated to the God Amun. It was steeped in history and had the most amazing views over the oasis palm tops also. It was interesting to see that the three highest points in Siwa were believed to be linked by underground tunnels. When I stood at the highest point to the

Temple of the Oracle, intuitively I felt the connection between these three mountains.

Further down the road were the remains of the Temple of Umm Ubayd which was once connected with the Temple of the Oracle. Still further on is the most famous spring, Cleopatra's bath. Despite the green looking water, there are bubbles and you can swim there.

It was now early afternoon and Hossam was about to drive back to Cairo and would meet up with us in Bahariya tomorrow afternoon. It was another long day for him and I hoped he would make it home safely.

After lunch, I wanted to walk into the township to look around and to have a coffee. There weren't many tourists here and I didn't know the way so I thought I'd ask Ahmed if he would walk with me, which he did. Along the way, a group of children ran up to us asking for money. We declined and I thought of the boy with his shop at Shali and regretted not buying something from him.

I had a great time wandering the streets with Ahmed, looking at the houses and shops and just getting a general feel for life here. We found a cafe and filled in some time talking about our lives, about life in Egypt and Siwa and just people watching. My highlight was seeing a donkey and cart that had a sign saying "taxi for hire". This was the most authentic taxi I have seen in my life and I wondered if it was a sign of the future.

Siwa is a great mix of the modern with the old, from the car to the donkey and cart, from the locals, some women completely covered except for their eyes to the tourist in t-shirt and shorts. It was such a land of contrasts.

Chapter 9

BAHARIYA

It was another early morning start in preparation for our 400km drive to Bahariya. I had set my alarm for 5am and was awake to hear the Islamic "call to prayer" so I stayed in bed enjoying listening to the sacredness of the call. After my yoga, shower and meditation, I was glad that I had pushed back our 7am start time to 7.30am so that I could get some breakfast. Something had shifted in me and I didn't feel my normal happy self today.

In Siwa, they have their own language here so the chef had difficulty understanding what I meant by two fried eggs. When English is a second language, the challenge is to find ways of explaining things simply. I was struggling with the words and the gestures. Luckily, one of the tour drivers could see what was going on and came to my rescue by translating for me. I hadn't intended to eat more eggs although it was just about a ritual by now, but there was nothing else that I liked, not for breakfast anyway.

Just as I was finishing up, Ahmed came in. His plate was piled high with food which looked like he hadn't eaten for days. Jokingly I said, "didn't you have dinner last night" and he replied "no". I realized it wasn't funny and that my words lacked sensitivity. Why hadn't he eaten? I was puzzled.

I went back to my room to pack my bags. I sat on the bed and out of the blue, I had an overwhelming sense that I just wanted to go home. I felt a deep sadness within me and the tears poured out from my eyes. I didn't want to be here anymore. I didn't know why I was here, what the purpose of being here was and why I had spent so much money on this trip. I felt lost. Time was ticking by. I pulled myself together and checked out.

Humza, our driver was waiting for us with the four wheel drive. As we left Siwa, we passed many children on their way to school. Some were walking but most were being driven by their fathers on the donkey and cart. It was so cool to see.

Humza pointed a few things out on the way which Ahmed then converted to English for me. We passed the salt lakes and seeing the salt all sparkly and white was beautiful. It looked like diamonds on the ground. A bit further on, the sand was more of a brown color and he explained that they use this sand to build their houses. Then we were on long stretches of road, most of it in good condition. I didn't realize that for most of the trip, we would be driving on the road and that the new sections were like driving on a highway.

Humza drove fast and with the fast beat Egyptian music that was playing, I thought this is crazy. This whole trip now seemed crazy. And again I wondered why I was here and why was I doing this. The drive was like a race to get to the end, to Bahariya and I was being driven as fast as we could go with no time to just enjoy the experience, to step out into the desert. It wasn't what I was expecting.

I came to realize that Humza was a metaphor for how I had lived most of my life - at high speed, always in a rush to get to the destination and never taking the time to enjoy the journey. This had all changed a few years ago when I came to realize how unhappy and unfulfilled I was in my life. It was the start of many changes, much inner reflection and much personal learning and growth. I had to find the real me that had got lost in the superficial life I was living and that had brought me to Egypt a year ago.

Suddenly the tears and sadness came back. I wasn't sure why I was feeling like this but had the wisdom to know that something was being released, that this was an energetic clearing and that this would pass. I didn't want Humza or Ahmed to see my tears so I remembered the advice of a friend of mine Angelique, who told me to look up if you didn't want to cry. And that's what I did until I noticed that Humza was watching me intently. After a while, I started to feel uncomfortable and decided to strategically move out of the rear vision mirror and sit more on the right hand side of the vehicle.

Looking up and out of the window, the cloud formations caught my eye and I was blessed to see a big angel following us. In fact, I am sure there were many as every now and then I would see the most beautiful cherubs. Intuitively I knew I was in safe hands and that the energy here in the Desert was strong, powerful and purifying. I was finally letting go of some old sadness that no longer served me and the energies of the desert were supporting me in this process.

We stopped to alter the pressure of the tyres so we could drive on the sand dunes. As I stepped out of the car to stretch my legs, I saw a bubble float past me and land near my feet. Then I saw another land on me and I knew I was around orbs. Wow, I thought, how cool is that, I can see them in daylight; normally I only see them at night. That lifted my spirits – I loved it here and loved being in this energy which was so pure.

We continued our drive with some of it being very bumpy. Suddenly I felt very tired and as soon as I closed my eyes, I went into a deep sleep. It happened so fast that I knew I was going through an energetic shift. When I wake from these shifts, I feel incredibly clear and it was a good thing that I did as we hit some bad spots on the road and we all literally bounced around the vehicle.

There were many military checkpoints throughout the drive. At one checkpoint, the staff picked some flowers for me which I thought was really sweet. Not much grows in the desert and the leaves were very fragrant. I knew it was a herb but I couldn't remember which one. At another checkpoint, we were asked if we could take one of the men to Bahariya with us as there was no transport for him. The luggage was rearranged to make room for him and he climbed in the back amongst our bags. I felt sorry for him and had no idea why he was not allowed to take a seat in the vehicle.

We continued driving and Humza asked if I wanted to stop for lunch. I was not expecting lunch and didn't realize that he had brought lunch for us. We pulled up on a sand dune. Out came an Egyptian rug and he prepared a very simple but totally tasty lunch for us. It consisted of three dishes: tuna, tomato, Spanish onion and lemon juice; tomato and feta cheese; tuna and Lebanese cucumber served with the Egyptian version of pita bread. It looked wonderful but I didn't know how to eat it so Ahmed introduced me to the Egyptian way of eating which is with your hands. It was awesome – a picnic in the desert – I loved it. This was another one of those surreal moments when I was truly grateful to be here and in the moment.

We had been traveling for about seven hours and it wasn't far from here to Bahariya. As we approached Bahariya, I instantly loved it. It was a small town of around 18,000 people and we were staying at the International Hot Spring Hotel, which is also fantastic. I loved meeting Peter the owner, who was someone who has a genuine interest in people and comes out to greet his guests, often knowing them by first name. The staff were really friendly and hospitable. I felt that Peter knew how to run a great business and I immediately felt at home, knowing that one night was not going to be long enough here.

The hotel borders on the Black Mountain which was like a giant magnet to me. Peter explained that just outside the hotel grounds, there were some stairs that I could take to climb up and enjoy the view. And so with my camera, I was off to explore the sights. It was an easy climb up, thanks to the stairs, and I found a rock to sit on. It was so peaceful here and the energy so good that I decided it would be nice to do a meditation. No sooner had I closed my eyes when I was greeted by Atlantis, a new spiritual guide who spoke to me in an old English dialect. He said:

"Blessed is thee that maketh the journey and thou has maketh the journey, we rejoice and honor thee".

What he meant by these words was the willingness and courage to take the inner journey to personal growth, development and self-mastery. He told me of some ancient teachings that I now had access to and that this was once my home that I had ruled here and these were my people. He told me to open my eyes and look at everything around me. He then showed me a vision of my true potential and an image of how, through fear, I had chosen to keep myself small.

He said "it is time for you to take your place in the world. Do not be afraid. You are a leader and you will lead with wisdom and love in your heart". Tears of love and joy poured from my eyes as I was blessed in this beautiful energy of pure unconditional love from my spiritual guides. It was a moving experience and one I knew I would never forget. I now knew why I was here, what the purpose of this trip was and I also knew this was a journey I had to make on my own. I needed the space and time to find more of me, the real me and to continue to open my heart to love, understanding and compassion that only Egypt, my spiritual homeland could offer.

I walked back to the hotel intending to write down as much as I could remember about what Atlantis had told me. Near Reception, one of the staff, Mahoumed, started a conversation with me about the spring and the spa pool. He told me that the water in the spa pool was indeed from an underground hot spring. To prove his point he said "come with me and I will show you" and I was off on another mini adventure. We walked out of the hotel grounds and within a few minutes, we were at the source of the hot water which was being pumped back to the hotel. I was amazed at how hot the water was (around 45 degrees Celsius) and he assured me it was very therapeutic. Mahoumed offered to take my photo which he did and on the way back told me about the area and the hotel. He pointed to his motorbike and said I will take you for a tour of Bahariya and I thought this sounded like great fun. But then I also thought Ahmed would not be pleased with me if I hadn't told him where I was going and I wasn't sure how much this would cost, especially given my memories of my day at the Pyramids. I declined, for now anyway.

It was hot here and the best time to soak in the spa was after dinner and that's what I did. The water was actually orange due the iron content and full of minerals reminding me of the mud pools back home in Rotorua. It was deeply relaxing, but also extremely hot that I doubt I stayed in more than five minutes. It was the perfect finish to the day.

The next day, I had intended to go back up to Black Mountain to meditate before we left. I had bought a wonderful Western Desert map from Reception and over breakfast, Ahmed and I talked about the sites to visit in the next few days. My itinerary was lacking some of the things I wanted to do and I knew it was my fault that I hadn't been specific enough when I had made the bookings. But I also wanted to find a solution that would meet everyone's needs. And that's what we did. But it took longer than I expected and so I ran out of time to go back up Black Mountain. Although disappointed, I knew that my connection to Bahariya was so strong that I'd only need to close my eyes and I would be back here again. It was etched in my heart and I intuitively knew that I would return again soon.

As I was checking out, I found a fantastic book called "Desert Songs" by Arita Baaijens. Arita is an environmentalist from Holland and one day the 'desert called' and she left her home to travel alone with her small caravan of camels to explore the Egyptian and Sudan deserts. I admired her courage. On the back cover, I read these words:

"It is a story about an inward journey, a rite of passage. It's about leaving the world you know to venture into the unknown where you discover your true strength. How strong are you when there's no back up? Where do your limits lie?"

This was her story, her voyage of discovery. The experience changed her life and I came to understand that like her, this was my story, my voyage of discovery and that as I was changing, so too would my life.

Bahariya had become famous for the Golden Mummies which were only discovered here in 1996 when legend had it, that a donkey stumbled on a hole near the Temple of Alexander The Great. The rider looked down to see a golden mummy staring at him in the sand and this was the beginning of an important archaeological discovery. In what's known as the Valley of the Mummies, over 10,000 mummies have since been found. There is a small museum here where you can view the mummies, some of which have incredibly well-preserved gold faces, breast plates and inscriptions. Some of the smaller ones resemble children and they truly are small.

From here, we visited the two 26th dynasty tombs – Zed Amun Luf Ankh and his son Bannentiu. These magnificent tombs were buried deep into the earth. Access is by way of steep stairs to a very small entrance. Inside there was only room for a few people at a time and yet they were stunning – the art on the walls truly beautiful. Although you cannot take photos inside, I said to Ahmed that I'd love to take a photo of these so that I could paint them when I am at home.

As we left Bahariya, we passed a few women out doing their shopping. They were dressed traditionally, fully covered from head to toe with just their eyes showing. Similar to Greece, the food is bought and prepared fresh each day and this was something that made good sense to me and something I decided I would do more of when I returned home.

We were back on the road again with about 500kms ahead of us. It felt good to be in the desert, even though the days and distances were long. I still revered the scenery, the beauty and expansiveness of it as well as the purity of the energy here. We listened to Shirin, the Egyptian singer, Elissa the Lebanese singer and then Celine Dion, a voice I knew.

Hossam and Ahmed were in top form and they decided to teach me some Egyptian words. 'Salam Alikom' is a greeting you hear all the time which means 'peace on you'. They would say this every time we went through a checkpoint or met someone new. The reply is 'Alikom salaam' which literally means 'on you peace'. Then there's 'maa salama' which is 'goodbye with peace'. Wow, I thought these were incredibly respectful ways of greeting another person, something we have lost in the western world.

About halfway to the Farafra Oasis is Crystal Mountain which you cannot miss as it is literally on the side of the road. We climbed up the mountain which is crystal quartz and was huge. I took lots of photos but the sunlight and the reflection were so strong that they didn't come out. Everywhere you look the light is reflected back to you and it's like a sea of diamonds. The energy here was pure, strong and powerful and as these crystals sit in the sun all day, they are fully charged with energy.

It was about lunchtime when we arrived at Farafra, another small oasis. A number of children were walking home from school for lunch and they were very curious to see me here. Hossam took us to a local cafe and we had another traditional Egyptian lunch. In fact, they made so much food for us that we couldn't finish it all. I asked Ahmed what they do with the leftovers and he said that often it is given to those who are very poor. That was another thing I liked about here, people are very thoughtful about not wasting food. Again, not something that we do so well in the western world.

Back on the road again, it was another 300kms to Dakhla and we passed people on their way home from work, typically by donkey, horse or motor bike. As the dusk turned to darkness, it was hard to see all the traffic on the road, especially as the Egyptians turn their headlights off and switch on their indicators when another car is approaching. I wondered how many animals were injured through road accidents.

It was pitch black when we arrived at Dakhla. The hotel was like a mosque all lit up and built into the side of a hill. On first impressions, this looked like a five star hotel and it was. As we walked to my room, I looked up to the night sky. There was a slither of the moon, what looked like millions of stars until I did a second take and realized they were orbs. How awesome it was to be in this energy. I was once again at home, I loved it here, it was so peaceful and it felt abundant.

There were many rooms at this hotel but hardly anyone was here. It appeared there were only five in use. When I went for dinner, I was the only one there, so I asked if I could sit outside under the stars as they prepared the meal. This was a magic spot.

When dinner was served, I went inside. I usually don't mind eating on my own. In fact you get used to it when you travel a lot but I did feel quite lonely being the only person in the entire restaurant and for some reason, we had problems conversing in English so there really wasn't anyone to talk to. The staff served me a huge meal which was totally delicious but I couldn't eat it all so I left a lot behind. Afterwards, I went back to my room and sat outside under the stars, soaking up the beauty, tranquility and peacefulness. It was a magic night, a romantic spot in many ways, and I thought how nice it would have been to have had someone to share this moment with.

Chapter 10

DAKHLA

I knew it was 5am when I heard the "call to prayer" and I wondered why my alarm hadn't gone off. My head felt heavy and I felt very tired today. It was still dark and I decided that I'd lie in bed a bit longer. Then my alarm did go off, I switched on the light intending to get up, but I didn't have any energy.

When I did get up, it was after 6am and I had a dreadful headache, a bit like I had been hit over the head and I guessed it was the effects of dehydration. These last few days we had been driving for long hours through the desert and as there were no toilets, I had decided to drink less to last the distance. Now I was paying the price.

In the daylight, I could see that the hotel was built like a mosque, incredibly ornate and artistically designed, yet with wonderful simplicity. I loved the French doors that led out to the built-in seats on the balcony with the big comfy cushions and the magnificent views to the green pastures with the cows, donkeys and horses, another contrast to the desert.

Although the hotel looked very new, ironically there were no face cloths in the bathroom but I did have a basin with a plug. The shower was very modern with only one small problem, I couldn't get any hot water so I had a cold shower today which was actually, quite refreshing.

Once again, I was the only person at the restaurant and the staff had trouble understanding my English. Forever polite, we tried to find a way to understand each other. Breakfast consisted of a range of cheeses, Egyptian bread, honey, jam, tea and coffee, and of course a knife and fork which is for the tourist as Egyptians eat with their hands. But there were no fried eggs today!

I went back to my room to zip up my luggage and as I turned to take it towards the door, I was surprised to find a man standing there. He was one of the porters and although I didn't ring for help, he intuitively knew. He was a very gentle man, but again we had trouble conversing. I tried to tell him to take the bags and I'd be there in a minute which he didn't comprehend so I pointed for him to go which he did.

I took my key back to Reception and then tried to find the porter to give him his tip. But I could not find him, so sadly he missed out. Wages are very low here, everyone tips and everyone depends on the tipping. I didn't appreciate this when I was here last year in the way that I understand it now. In Greece, there are no porters which means that you carry your own luggage, often up very narrow and steep stairs. After a few times of doing this, everyone on the tour became very grateful to the work that the porters do and the few dollars you spend is really worth it. It's a win-win for everyone.

It was 8am and Hossam and Ahmed were waiting for me. I felt there was something different about them today, almost like something wasn't right but I didn't know what it was. Today we were driving to Luxor which was about 700kms away. But first we had a few local stops.

We took a tour of El Kasr which is the Old Islamic City here in Dakhla. It was extensive with lots of alleyways to keep cool from the summer heat and the sand storms, ancient houses with heavy wooden doors, a mosque, a school that also once served as a courtroom, an olive press and corn mill and even a place where people used to be hung. Our local guide Halim pointed to the front door of a house and proudly told us that his great grandfather lived there. There was something magical about Halim, he touched my heart and I felt an instant connection with him. El Kasr had a great feel about it, a real community spirit and I could imagine myself living here.

One thing I loved about so many of the Egyptian people I met were their radiant smiles, their humbleness, gentleness and gratitude. Great guides, particularly those in these small rural areas, really enjoyed taking the time to show you around and they really wanted to make sure that you understood everything they were saying. There is no rush and they will happily answer your questions. In essence, they are proud to be of service and Halim was very much like this.

We had finished our tour and I wasn't sure what was going on when Ahmed raced off to find Hossam, without tipping Halim. Halim looked worried that he wouldn't be paid and I sensed his disappointment.

But he didn't have to worry as Ahmed just needed to get some money from Hossam. I said thank you to Halim and thought how much this man reminded me of my late grandfather and how nice it would be if we could just sit and talk over a cup of tea, when a young girl nearby heard me say thank you and began imitating my accent. It was both delightful and funny.

From here, we drove in search of the Deir el-Hagar Temple. We stopped a few times to check on directions and I noticed that the local people were always genuinely happy to assist.

Again, we had a really helpful local guide Jabir, who was keen to make sure I understood what he was saying and the temple itself was just fabulous. It was dedicated to Amun, Mut, Khonsu and Horus. This was the main temple in the Roman period and was built between 30 B.C. – A.D. 396 and had since been restored. Not far from here, you could see the tombs and the remains of houses so like most things, my sixth sense told me there is much more buried beneath the sand. As we were leaving, a group of German tourists turned up and I was reminded to be grateful to have been able to explore these sites on our own, without the crowds that you get at the well-known temples. This was truly off the beaten track and that's what made it so fantastic for me.

On the way back, we had to stop in Dakhla to get the papers sorted for the next leg of our journey through the desert. We stopped outside a restaurant and Ahmed told me that they hadn't eaten breakfast yet so he would get the breakfast while Hossam would take me to the Tourism Police to do the paperwork. It is ironic that we are told as tourists not to let our passport out of our sight, but in Egypt that's impossible and I wondered now, how many photocopies there were of me.

It was mid morning and we went back to pick up Ahmed. I asked him why they hadn't eaten breakfast and he told me that they had slept in the van last night because they had run out of money for a room. I wished they had told me earlier as I hadn't paid them their tips and maybe that would have helped. They didn't have any dinner either and I felt sorry for them, especially given the meal I was served last night which was so generous that I am sure all three of us could easily have shared it. But the thing was if I had known, I would have bought them dinner anyway; you just would.

There is a lot to understand about the Egyptian way of life and how people are paid here and so I asked Ahmed a whole lot more questions. It reminded me to be grateful for all that I have in my life and that my cold shower this morning was irrelevant in the bigger scheme of things. I was starting to really understand that a lot of things in life actually aren't that important in reality.

Our drive took us east to El Kharga. On the way, we stopped at the Rock of Inscriptions where Hossam showed us how to carve our names onto the rock. He wrote his in Egyptian including his nickname Zatona and I wrote mine in English.

We continued driving and Hossam had some local music on and I found myself once again feeling sleepy. As I closed my eyes and drifted off, I remembered hearing every word in the songs and although I was asleep, I was also awake and conscious of everything going on around me. I knew that this was another energetic shift. When I opened my eyes, we were coming up to another checkpoint.

Ahmed had fallen asleep too and I thought he seemed very tired today. Hossam and I were joking about Ahmed being asleep when he woke up. He curtly told us that he didn't sleep at all last night because of three mosquitoes. I thought he wasn't himself today and now I knew why. That made me wonder if Hossam got any sleep and so I asked him and fortunately he did. I had a feeling that Hossam could probably sleep anywhere. He was one of those people who always seemed happy, was always smiling and he took everything in his stride.

Even so, I did feel for these guys. This was a long journey and I wondered how you could be at your best when you hadn't eaten or slept properly. By the time they would drop me off in Luxor, they would be continuing through the night to Cairo which was another seven hours at best. I think Hossam would have driven for more than 16 hours today and he had an airport pick up the next day at 10am.

There were many tourist and military checkpoints to pass through on our journey. By now, checkpoints had become a joke between us. Normally what would happen when we pulled over was that they would ask Hossam the time and then ask where I was from. Hossam would tell them New Zealand. They didn't know where that was so they would ask him again. Still not knowing where NZ was, they would then take a look at me through the window as if I was literally from another planet. By then, we would all start laughing. There would be another exchange in Arabic that I didn't understand but I knew it was funny. The closest most people got were the Netherlands. It seemed that New Zealanders are a rare breed in this part of the world and I thought maybe next time I could bring a NZ flag and a world map!

We arrived in El Kharga, the busiest and largest town in the Western Desert. Hossam drove us to the Hibis Temple which was built in the 25th dynasty and dedicated to Amun. We pulled into the drive only to find that the temple was closed. They told me to come back in three years' time when it would be open, which made me laugh. Nevertheless, Ahmed said something and they agreed to let me in to walk around and take a few photos. It reminded me of the temples I saw in Greece.

Back on the road again, I noticed the change in the landscape. There was something magical about the desert, the golden sand contrasted with the blue sky and the straight black road that goes on forever.

Sometimes the desert was flat, sometimes mountainous, sometimes with greenery. But it was always changing, just like life really. But it still felt like we were driving on an ancient seabed.

As dusk approached, I noticed the large shadows that fell across the mountains. It reminded me that we all have our shadow self, the part that we either deny its presence or the part that we are not yet aware of. Our personal growth comes from embracing the shadow self, understanding what it is teaching us and choosing to act with higher levels of awareness.

We witnessed another stunning sunset. I tried to capture it on film as it was such a vibrant red glow but as the sun sets quickly, it was a bit hit and miss. As we got closer to Luxor, we again passed many farmers coming home from work with the donkey and cart as the main form of transportation. There were even shepherds, who so gently herded their sheep with just a stick to another pasture. It was unbelievable how calm the sheep were given they were competing with the cars, donkeys and motorbikes who shared the same busy road.

The volume of traffic substantially increased which was something that we hadn't experienced in the towns across the desert. I found myself having to adjust again from the expanse and almost solitude of the desert to the busyness of modern day city life.

Ahmed told me that a new guide Michael was waiting for me at the hotel. As we got closer, it dawned on me that this might be the last time that I would see Hossam and Ahmed. It was a weird feeling as we had journeyed over 2,000kms together in just five days. Having spent so much time in each others company, I realized they had become very special to me and it felt sad to say goodbye. They were very easy men to be with and I had loved every minute of it. I knew I would miss them and I also knew I was grateful to have shared the journey with them. It was nearly 6pm. They still had a long drive back to Cairo and as we said goodbye, I silently asked the angels to oversee and divinely protect them on the long drive home.

I checked into the hotel and got a text message from Rosemary, my NZ friend who lives here in Egypt. She was in Luxor with two other New Zealanders and we agreed to catch up over dinner. She suggested the Steigenberger Nile Palace Hotel and to my delight, I discovered it was the hotel I had stayed in last year. It brought back wonderful memories of my time here when I started each day at six in the morning, sitting beside the Nile meditating in the peace and tranquility. Then at night, Aroha my roommate and I would stay up talking till all hours. We got on so well that I kept feeling that she was like a sister to me.

Over dinner, we each shared our experiences of the last week. As I talked, I realized how happy I was feeling. I knew something significant had shifted in me by being in the desert, knowing again that I was meant to take this journey alone. I could feel that I had changed, that I wasn't the same person that had arrived in Cairo ten days ago. The "desert had called me home" and I was now at home with who I am. I had found another part of the real me and I knew that both Hossam and Ahmed had helped me in ways I couldn't fully comprehend.

I was blessed to have had both Hossam and Ahmed. They were "gentle men" in the widest sense of the word and very subtlely, they had touched my heart. They showed me honor, respect, they were thoughtful to my needs, they made me laugh, they shared their worlds with me through their music, songs, stories and our conversations. I had seen and felt the world through their eyes and it was a very humbling experience as they had taught me a lot about themselves, the Egyptian people and the culture here. They were easy to be with; Hossam was always smiling and it comes from his heart and Ahmed had enthusiasm that was contagious; he was always smiling too. They deepened my understanding, humility and compassion.

When I went to bed it was about 10.30pm. My mind turned to them and I wondered where they were. Did they stop for dinner?

Were they safe? Were they OK? And how much longer before they would get to bed? I missed them.

Chapter 11

LUXOR

The city of Luxor is one of my favorite places in Egypt. It was going to be an action packed day so once again I got up at 5am to do some yoga, knowing just how much I needed to stretch after all the long hours of traveling that I had done.

We were to leave at 7.30am but I was ready early so I went and stood outside the hotel. It was much busier here and I found it hard to adjust too after all the small towns I had just visited. As I waited, I noticed how hot it already was, which was surprising given that this was the start of their winter. Numerous taxis pulled up and I waved them on.

My guide for the day was David who spoke superb English. I explained to him that although we were here to visit the temples on the East and West Bank, I also needed to go to the Sunshine Orphanage to donate the art materials and to Animal Care of Egypt to donate some bandages that I had brought with me. I wasn't sure where these places were but I figured they would be nearby. He said that we would go to the West Bank first and then, to the Sunshine Orphanage, which was on the way back to the Karnak Temple. We would be there late morning. That was perfect as the orphanage had told me to visit there before 12pm or after 2pm so this would work well.

As we were driving, David and I talked some more and I explained to him that 'giving back' and social responsibility were important aspects of my work. I told him I was looking for an orphanage that I could work alongside with the intention of building a long term relationship and that I was particularly interested in helping orphaned children. He listened intently and I knew he understood what I was saying. Then he said, if I was interested, he could take me to another orphanage, one for disabled children and also abandoned elderly people. He asked me if I would like to go there. "Yes", I said "I'd love to". It turned out that David helps out there when he has no paid work and also in his spare time. Wow, I thought, I most certainly had found the right person to help me.

The drive to the Valley of the Kings and Queen Hatshepsut's Temple is about thirty minutes as they are located on the West Bank and we had to cross the Nile. As we got closer to the Valley of the Kings, I could feel the energy of the mountains calling me home. It was like a magnetic pull and I just loved these moments as I never know when or where they would happen.

I stepped out of the car soaking up the beauty and sacredness of this place. It was even more stunning than I remembered. Indeed, it felt like a great honor to be here once again. There are 62 tombs here that you can visit although it is commonly believed there are many yet to be discovered. However, a number of the tombs are often closed for renovation work as this is done in the winter months which just so happens to coincide with the peak tourist season. Typically you purchase one ticket that allows you to visit three tombs.

At first, I wanted to go back and see the tombs that I visited last year as they were so amazing, yet I also felt I would be disappointed as I had come to realize that my energy had changed so much from last year, that the places that had resonated with me then didn't have the same feel now. I asked David for his suggestion. He suggested that I visit the tombs of Ramses 1st, 3rd and 9th and that's what I did, although next time I thought I'd buy two tickets and do six tombs as three never felt like enough.

The Valley of the Kings is one of the busiest tourist sites with something like 15,000 people visiting here a day in peak season and it is therefore common to queue. I was thrilled when I walked straight into the tomb of Ramses 1st with no queues and to find just a few German tourists inside. Although this was a small tomb, the paintings on the walls were sensational. I was drawn to one of the gods who was holding a shepherd's crook and the scepter that were identical to a drawing my friend Mary had done for me. I needed to know which god it was and so I looked at the various visitors wondering if I could approach one of them, but that didn't feel right. So I asked the guard who very kindly gave me a complete guided tour of the entire art and the inscriptions. Usually when they do this, they will ask you for money and I was more than happy to pay him for doing a lot more than just answering my question, but he didn't ask. It was an interesting thing that for most of my time in Egypt, the people who genuinely helped me never asked for money and yet those who were less than genuine always put their hand out.

It turned out it was the God Amun-Ra and with my question answered, I wondered what the significance was, if any, and the relevance to the drawing I had at home. As I was about to leave, there was suddenly a very large queue to get in and so, I was once again blessed to know that it was perfect and divinely timed that I had this experience on my own.

Outside of the tombs, there is a constant stream of people trying to sell you books, postcards and just about anything. I found them pushy and again, it was the contrast of being alone in the desert to now being in a major tourist site at a busy time. I entered Ramses 3rd, then the 9th the latter which had a really long queue. People had lost their patience with queuing and decided to enter via the exit. This created heated arguments with those who had patiently waited their turn and I found it impossible to meditate in front of the tomb. People pushed passed me and eventually I just had to get out of there and I felt angry that people did not respect these ancient sacred burial sites in the same way I did. I went to find David.

On the opposite side of the Valley of the Kings lies Queen Hatshepsut's Temple. Again this was a busy site and although it was only 9.30am, being in a valley with no wind or shade, it was very hot. In summer, the temperatures easily reach 45 degrees Celsius which most tourists cannot tolerate.

David told me that it was here that one of the most significant terrorist attacks occurred in 1997. Armed men came over the top of the mountain and started shooting, killing about 60 tourists before finally killing themselves. There are now armed guards stationed on the mountain and he pointed them out to me. This event led to armed escorts that were put in place for all tourists traveling by road for almost 11 years and that travels could only be made between 6am and 6pm. I thought how my trip through the desert would have been different if this had still been in place now.

David left me alone to enter and explore the temple at my own pace and this was something that I really appreciated. I immediately connected with the big statues of Queen Hatshepsut. I loved standing in front of them and feeling the strength and power of her energy.

I went to another part of the temple. There were no other tourists around when the security guard came over to me and was being very helpful in showing me where to stand to take the best photos and before long; he followed me everywhere, engaging me in any conversation. As I was about to leave, he put his hand out for money, requesting a tip for being helpful and I realized once again how naive I had been. When I told David what happened, he was disappointed that he hadn't warned me. I told him not to worry, it was my own fault and I saw the funny side to it. I was still mastering discernment just like Ahmed had told me when I first arrived.

From here, we traveled back across the Nile to the East Bank and found the Sunshine Orphanage. This was set up by a British woman called Pearl Smith in 1992 and they had just moved into their new purpose built premises, caring for around 85 abandoned children. The buildings were exquisite, more modern than even some of the buildings back home.

I was introduced to Mary, an English lady that helped out here and I gave her the rather large bag of art materials that many of my friends and clients had gifted to help the children. Mary offered to show me around. We started with a tour of the pre-school and nursery which was impressive, very Western and practical. The pre-school had three teaching rooms plus an art room, a computer room and a sewing room. I met the art teacher and the children in her class and knew that the art materials would be put to good use here.

Mary told me that the children had never had an outside play area and so naturally they had never played outside. I found that quite hard to comprehend especially coming from a place like NZ. In this new facility, they had green grass which in itself is a rarity in Egypt and slides and swings, the typical things you would expect to see in most people's backyards at home. Despite a rough start to life, these children were certainly being given a great chance now.

Our next visit was to the Good Samaritan Orphanage and this was a complete contrast to the Sunshine Orphanage. We entered a very old building that had 3 floors. This orphanage looks after disabled and elderly people who had been abandoned by their families. David explained that one Egyptian man had started this on his own. They now have 28 children on one floor and on the second floor were 20 elderly people. They were hoping to rent the third floor in the near future which they planned to make into a school for the children.

Everything here was very basic and it was the basic things that they needed the most like food, clothing, bedding, toys, cleaning and of course, love. There are 14 girls who work here and the love they exude for the children and the old people is moving. David took me everywhere showing me the bedrooms where 4 or 5 children would sleep, to the TV room where about 6 children were crowded in a small room in the dark watching children's movies and he introduced me to everyone along the way.

Up on the third floor, I met two disabled children who moved me in a way that words could not describe. The first child was actually a 32 year old adult, but he was a dwarf. He put his hand out to greet me and as I held his hand, I felt the pure love in his heart. He radiated the most heart warming smile, genuinely so pleased to meet me which brought tears of compassion to my eyes. The other child had a greater level of disabilities. His body was twisted like a piece of metal, yet somehow he shuffled towards me determined that he would shake my hand and say hello too. I took his hand, said hello and I found myself overwhelmed with emotions trying to understand how we could abandon another human being.

Being in their presence for just those brief few moments, I knew in my heart that I had found what I was looking for and these children had filled me with a purity of love that I knew I just wanted to do something to help them. I knew this would be the orphanage that I would support and work alongside, developing a long term relationship to support their needs. I was so grateful to have had David with me and this experience became the catalyst in deciding to write and self-publish this book as a way of raising money to help fund their school to support their special needs.

Leaving here to go to the Karnak Temple was quite heart wrenching.

The Karnak Temple is one of the largest outdoor temples in the world. There is so much to see and explore here. David gave me a detailed explanation of the many areas, explaining the history and meaning to me. It was now midday and very hot so we decided to take a break in the shade of the cafe. I bought David a cold drink and we talked about life in general. He told me he was about to get married and was hoping to have the engagement party this weekend. Then his face dropped and his heart sank as he told me that the respective families were fighting and he was not sure if the wedding would go ahead at all. Marriages are still arranged here and I was not sure if this was an arranged marriage or not, but I did know that David absolutely loved this woman. I felt really sorry for him, trying to imagine how it must feel to love someone but your family won't allow you to marry them. In many ways the Egyptian people do not enjoy the freedom we take for granted every day in the western world.

David went on to tell me that the biggest reason for divorce in Egypt is always because of the families. I sensed his frustration so I suggested to him to close his eyes and imagine everything being resolved peacefully, that both families were in harmony with each other and to see himself being married on his wedding day. I was teaching him the spiritual concept that we create our own reality so what we think is what we create. Therefore you must envision what you want and hold it in your mind's eye, in your heart and most of all, learn to trust and to have faith. I suggested to him to keep his thoughts positive and on what he wanted in his life.

Just then, his phone rang and ironically he told me it was his fiancée. When David got off the phone, he immediately said, "isn't that funny that we were just talking about her and she rang". Of course, I knew this was no coincidence. These two were divinely connected to each other and she picked up on the energy of our conversation. I knew that they were meant for each other, that they both loved each other deeply and I felt certain the wedding would go ahead. David just needed to have faith.

We left the cafe and agreed on a time to meet near the entrance so I could explore the temple on my own. I wandered around many monuments of Ramses and I wanted to sit and meditate in front of him, but away from the crowds and preferably, in the shade. No sooner did I have this thought when I found the perfect spot, a rock to sit on, right in front of a huge monument of him and in the shade. I closed my eyes and connected with his energy. I don't remember much or even how long I was there but I do remember being told that it was now time for me to find my voice, to be a voice and to speak up in the world. I felt a lot of energy being cleared from my throat chakra.

On our way back, we stopped at the Luxor Temple and this is truly one of my favorite sites. I really wanted to come here at night when it takes on a completely different form. However, I was blessed to be the only person here and to have had the temple all to myself. I was once again drawn to the statues of Ramses when I realized I had been working with his energy all day, in all the temples that I had been to. When I looked up at him, I always had the sense of his incredible power, strength and presence, yet he was peaceful and that was his message to me 'to fully stand in and own my power, strength and presence and to not be afraid of embracing it'.

Finally, to finish the tour, I had asked David to take me to Animal Care of Egypt which is a not for profit that supports the welfare of animals and is free to all Egyptian people. I had some bandages to donate and I was hoping that they would give me a tour of their premises so I could understand their work. Our driver wasn't sure where it was and the instructions I had were apparently incorrect so we stopped to ask for directions. It wasn't that difficult to find but when we got there, it was closed due to it being the weekend so we left the bandages with one of the staff at the gate. I was disappointed that I wouldn't be in Luxor when it would be open as this was a cause close to my heart and one I was particularly interested in understanding more about.

By the time I got back to the hotel, I felt emotionally exhausted from a day of such diverse experiences. It was mid afternoon and still incredibly hot and I made my way to the swimming pool to reflect on everything that had happened. Rosemary was still in Luxor so she sent me a text message inviting me to join her for dinner again with her clients. We agreed that I would meet them in the lobby of their hotel which was a five minute walk away.

I decided to wear my favorite dress to dinner tonight as we were celebrating Rosemary's birthday. I left the hotel and had just taken a few steps along the road when I was seriously hassled by a man. Normally when you put your hands up and keep walking, they will leave you alone and I walk so fast that most people can't keep up with me anyway. But not this man. He wanted me to go into his shop and I showed and told him "no" but he persisted, partly I thought, because I was a woman on my own. Suddenly, I felt a huge anger rise up in me and I very nearly turned to face him knowing that I would have screamed at him to leave me alone. At the same time and in a split second, I had a vision of him trying to feed his family. As quick as the anger flared, it was replaced with compassion and understanding, that just like everyone else on the planet, he just wanted to earn a living to have a better quality of life too. And although I didn't like the way he treated me, I realized it wasn't about me, I had understood why he was the way he was and I walked by in peace.

I waited in the lobby at Rosemary's hotel enjoying an interesting and hilarious conversation with a very young man who was selling Egyptian perfumes and oils. I wanted to buy some but didn't have enough time to decide so I told him I'd have to come back later. He said "I will wait for you, what time you come back"? I told him I didn't know and I wasn't even sure that I would come back today and I hoped he wouldn't wait all night.

The others turned up and we decided that before dinner, we had to visit the shop called Radwan, a well-known jeweler here in Luxor. I had been here last year and purchased an ankh, which is a sacred symbol for life. Back in Cairo the chain had broken and I needed a new one.

We walked into Radwans' interrupting what looked like an exciting World Cup soccer game that the staff were watching on a small TV. Rosemary introduced us to Hussein, a man I instantly connected with.

He intuitively selected a piece of jewelry that was unique to each of us. These were stunning handmade pieces ranging from gods, goddesses and sacred symbols, all exquisite in 18 carat gold.

I tried on just about everything he showed me and we had a lot of fun agreeing or disagreeing on what suited me. He kept telling me that each piece made me more beautiful and I would laugh. Of course, I didn't always agree with him, however he would try to sell me his point of view.

Hussein kept promising that when I come back to Egypt next time that he would marry me. He wasn't serious, he was just teasing and having fun and of course and I was playing along. When it finally came to ask the prices, the two pieces that I loved the most were just too expensive so I settled on a new gold chain for my ankh and told him that maybe next time I would buy one of the other pieces. He said with a big grin, "yes you must come back and I will give you a special price on your jewelry and it will be free if you marry me"! I laughed, thanked him for his great service and for the entertainment.

By now we were hungry as we had spent a lot of time at Radwans'. Hussein offered to help us get a horse and carriage to take us to a local restaurant for dinner. There were plenty to choose from, but unfortunately a verbal fight broke out amongst at least two of the owners as to who should take us. These men were really yelling at each other and many others joined in. Hussein, who was such a gentleman did not like this, neither did we and we very nearly opted for a taxi instead. But somehow it was resolved and we trotted in the carriage down the main road of Luxor to the restaurant. We had a wonderful night in a very typical Egyptian restaurant where the locals eat and our driver patiently waited for us to take us back to the hotel. They dropped me at my hotel first and as this would be the last time I would see these ladies in Egypt, I wished them well on the rest of their tour.

The next day I met up with Michael and a new driver to take me to the airport. Michael wanted to know how my tour had been yesterday and I told him it was fantastic and that David was totally awesome.

It seemed that they had been talking about me as Michael went on to say "you know, you are not the typical tourist. Instead of being at the temples, you want to spend all your time at the orphanages and the animal care places". I said "yes, that's true" and I was secretly proud of my new title of 'not being the typical tourist'.

Chapter 12

CAIRO AND HOMEWARD BOUND

It was a full flight from Luxor to Cairo and my bag was once again one of the first ones out. As with all my other airport transfers, Ahmed was there to meet me and take me to the hotel. He was smiling, full of energy and enthusiastically took my bags for me, welcoming me back to Cairo. It was good to see him again. I had become so used to traveling with Ahmed and Hossam through the desert that I had missed them in Luxor even though it was just two days since I had last seen them, it felt much longer. I asked Ahmed how the drive back from Luxor went. He said that they did stop for dinner, which I was pleased about as I had given them extra money, specifically for food. They had driven through the night, arriving in Cairo at five in the morning and Hossam had an airport pickup at 7am so he didn't have much of a rest or a break. Ahmed said he slept all of the next day.

As we arrived at the hotel, Ahmed handed me the company feedback form and asked me to fill it in. He said that I could give it back to him tomorrow when he would take me back to the airport.

Before I left Egypt, I knew I needed to find a present to take home for my daughter. I toyed with the idea of catching a taxi to the markets where I knew I could get things much cheaper than the shops at the hotel, but I wasn't sure how much it was going to cost to get there and also I was nearly out of money. In the end, I decided to buy from the hotel and negotiate with the shop owner.

At first, he wasn't that interested in giving me a lower price so it became a game when I picked up one of his maps, studied it carefully and then said the price was too much and that I had bought the same map in Bahariya for much less. He believed me (don't worry it was true) and from there we agreed on a few other items although in the end, he still wanted me to pay a little bit more and I wanted to pay a little bit less.

We were stuck until I told him that this was the only money I had left as I had already been to the cash flow machine to get the money out and he said "OK, I accept your offer". I said thank you, we shook hands and with a big smile, I told him I had really enjoyed shopping with him. He said he enjoyed it too and wished me safe travels.

With the shopping out of the way, I felt enticed to retire to the sun and swimming pool. At first, I was the only one there and it was so hot that it didn't take long before I was in the pool. I started reflecting on everything that had happened in the last two weeks, realizing just how much ground I had covered.

As I lay by the pool, I felt a great sense of sadness in my heart to be leaving here. I reflected on the diverse and varied experiences; from meeting my Bedouin guide Mohamed, who took me to a remote area at Mt Sinai where I found deep inner peace, to snorkeling the coral reef in the Red Sea, to being and understanding village life and poverty first hand in Cairo, to the call of the Desert – its beautiful vastness, spaciousness, and powerful energies, to the profound messages I received while sitting on Black Mountain in Bahariya, to sharing the Desert journey with Hossam and Ahmed and being with them, to the humble Egyptian people and guides who crossed my path and touched my heart, to the stunning orbs in Daklah, to the connection with Ramses at Luxor and to the disabled children and the orphanage that moved me in a way words couldn't describe. My eyes were filled with tears at the thought of leaving here, my spiritual home, yet I was incredibly grateful to have had this opportunity.

Later on when I was back in my room, I completed the feedback form that Ahmed had given me. Like so many feedback forms, it didn't really ask the real questions and although there was a space for comments, I had too many comments to write. I decided to find some paper and write a thank you letter to Ahmed and Hossam as they were the two people I had spent the most time with. I wanted them to know how much I had appreciated everything they had done for me. They ended up being two very long letters that I hoped they could understand. I sent Ahmed a text message and suggested that he meet me in the lobby before we left for the airport in the morning so I could give him my feedback face to face. Unfortunately, he couldn't text me back so I didn't know if he would be there or not.

I went for my last dinner with my faithful laptop as my companion and wrote solidly for three hours on this book. Most of this book had been written as it happened and yet, I would find there was always more to write, more to share, but I still wasn't ready to leave here.

Finally, my last day arrived. I checked out and waited for Ahmed in the lobby, but as I waited, I suddenly knew that he wasn't coming today. And I was right. I was greeted by a different guide who said that Ahmed wasn't able to make it and he had come instead. I was grateful now that I had taken the time to write the letters of thanks and so I asked this man if he could please give these letters to Ahmed for me which he promised he would do.

I met my driver who was Mohammad today, an older man who had driven for me before but I couldn't remember when. I knew there was one driver that I had forgotten to tip which was the first driver I had and I thought it was this man, but I wasn't sure. When we got to the airport, Mohammad got my bags out for me. I handed him the tip and as I did, he held both my hands, looked me directly in the eyes and said thank you. He then gave me a hug. I saw tears in his eyes and he kissed me on both cheeks and I felt in my heart, his genuine gratitude. He brought tears to my eyes too and I wondered what his life was really like. These are the people I love so much and they have taught me great humility and compassion. I was incredibly grateful for that moment, for the love and humility Mohammad shared with me and I wished I wasn't saying goodbye.

I know my work here is not finished. If anything, it has just begun and I know I will return again soon. Maybe even one day I may live here for a while but still, it wrenched my heart to be leaving and I had to hold back the tears as I walked into the airport to check in.

I was no longer the same person who arrived here two weeks ago. I had changed.

In Egypt, I had discovered another level of love, compassion, understanding, humility, gratefulness, peace, insight and inner growth. This was a journey that I was meant to take on my own and I know there will be many more journeys like this where I must walk the path alone. I remembered the words "blessed is the one that maketh the journey", and yes, I will always make the journey, for that is who I am.

And so it is, that I was blessed to have had this opportunity. I was blessed to have had such beautiful people cross my path and the wonderful friendships and relationships that I now have, and all that they knowingly and unknowingly have taught me. I have found more of the real me and I have gained a deep inner peace that I have never felt before.

And so, as they say in Egypt, *"Salam Alikom"* which means *"peace on you"* and *"maa salama"* which means *"goodbye with peace"*.

With much love
Joanne Hutchinson

Epilogue

I was in Egypt for 2 weeks in February 2010 and as always had the most interesting journey of self-discovery and personal growth. You may remember that I was there in October and one of the outcomes of that trip was the decision to self-publish my first book, as a way of raising funds for an orphanage that I want to help. It's all part of my commitment to 'giving back' and changing lives. I have been working on the book solidly for the last few months and so you can imagine how thrilled I was to receive the first 100 copies, which arrived at my front door a few days before I was to leave for Egypt again.

A day later, we discovered a problem with my beloved book. A few paragraphs had repeated themselves intermittently throughout the book and this now meant that a re-print was going to happen sooner than I had imagined. It seems the error occurred when the file was converted to a print ready file and I realized that it was my fault for not checking every page before accepting the final version. And so the greater purpose of this error was my opportunity to learn from this, and I knew intuitively that there would be another reason as to why the book had been delayed.

Egypt has long been considered a country of initiation; a place for personal discovery, growth and transformation. I love my time in Egypt and every trip has aided my personal growth, helping me to master important life lessons, understand my fears, understand what is important to me and to open my heart to greater love. In this trip, I was thrilled to be re-united with my friends Ahmed, Hossam, Amanda, David, and Hussein and to make new friendships with Amir, Sameh, Yvonne, Mustafa and Michael. Each of these people truly touched my heart, offering the most profound wisdom and insights for me personally and although I have thanked them for all that they have done for me, I doubt they fully comprehend the difference they have made to my life.

When I arrived in Cairo, I was greeted by Ahmed my local guide and Hossam my driver, both of whom I spent a lot of time travelling through the desert with last time. They taught me a lot about Egypt, the people and the culture, helping me to see and experience life through their eyes and not just a as a tourist staying in nice hotels and visiting the Temples. They helped me to see the other side of Egypt, the poverty, the wages, the long hours they work and taught me some Arabic that came in handy on this trip. I really enjoyed their company, they were easy to be with and we had a lot of fun along the way. Ahmed is brilliant at sorting everything out and Hossam, who is now married, remains my all-time favorite driver; he is a genius in the Cairo traffic. Seeing them and being welcomed by them at the airport made me feel like I had returned home.

The next day I met up with Amanda and Sameh. We had arranged to meet for lunch on the Nile, and then Sameh who is an Egyptologist was to take me to the Egyptian Museum which is totally fabulous by the way, then onto the Khan el Khalili Market.

I was here during school holidays and it was still peak tourist season so everywhere was super crowded and busy with people. As a consequence, the traffic was slow, like real slow and also it was nearing peak hour when we started to drive towards the market. Sameh and I talked along the way when out of the blue; he said "do you feel like an adventure"? He had a big grin on his face and so I said "yes". He said lets jump out of the van now and cross the road. Now crossing the road in Egypt, well the people give way to the cars and there are lanes but these are ignored by the drivers. It's like a race track, cars can pass you on either side and you make your own lanes here.

So here I was, leaping out of a van still moving, in peak hour traffic, with a driver in shock with what was happening and yelling out 'where are you going' and Sameh yelling back 'that he would call him later to tell him where to pick us up'. It was a lot of fun and the thought of whether the medical insurance would cover getting hit by a car briefly flashed through my mind yet there is something exciting about being spontaneous. And that's what this moment was. There was no fear, just total trust. And of course, the Egyptians do this every day!

At the market we stopped for coffee when I met the most beautiful young girl, probably not even 5 years old, who was selling beaded hats. She was so cute that I told Sameh I had to buy one for my daughter knowing that the money would go back to help her family. She took her time showing me her mobile shop, all the colors she had, gently placing each on one on the table for me to see. When I picked the orange one, she delightfully came over to put the hat on my head and ever so gently arranged it and my hair, so it was sitting perfectly on my head, in a way that only a child can do. She was ever so beautiful, radiating gentleness and love. We took some photos and she gave me a big hug and kiss as she left. She touched my heart, making me feel special and she made my day.

A few days later, I was in Luxor and spent time at the Good Samaritan Orphanage. David, my local guide introduced me to Ezzt who is the man who had the heart to set this orphanage up for disabled children and abandoned elderly people. This time, a number of the buildings around them had been demolished as the current Mayor has decided to re-invent the 3km Avenue of the Sphinxes that originally linked the Karnak Temple to the Luxor Temple. Any building or house in its way was demolished without the consent of the people. It is quite unbelievable. A huge mound of sand and rubbish greets you at the front door alongside a herd of goats.

Inside the orphanage, they have made great progress since I was here in October. I spent a number of hours meeting, talking to and holding hands with the children as well as with the staff. Meeting Ezzt was impressive, a gentle man that is called Father by all those here and he really is a father to them all, embracing them in so much love. They have now rented the 3rd floor of this building and have turned it into three school rooms. Ezzt told me that they now have other children who come from the villages for schooling during the day which is so fantastic. They have built a small gym which will help those with physical disabilities and he shared his vision for a new building which he is in the process of negotiating with a local church.

I was able to show him a copy of the original version of my book of which 33% of the proceeds will be donated to them and David translated the English into Arabic for him. He was very grateful for my support, offering me tea and allowing me to take the photos of the children which are now included in this edition.

Still in Luxor, I called into Radwan's which is one of the most amazing jewelers and gift shops here in Egypt, to buy some gifts. I met Hussein here last year and had a lot of fun negotiating with him and talking in general. He said he would marry me if I came back (don't worry, he was only joking) and still teases me that I should marry him. He offered me tea (the hospitality is something I love about the Egyptian way of life) and we talked, laughed and negotiated, all at the same time. When I complained about being hassled by the men here in Luxor, he became serious and started to give me some advice. He told me that I needed to draw a line in the sand and if anyone crossed it, he said you need to 'snap' back at them. He said it's all in the tone of your voice and that I must stand my ground and that I do not need to change who I am to be here. It was solid advice as it is all about personal power and setting boundaries and this was one of the lessons I soon came to realize that I was here to master. He said "here is my phone number and you call me for anything, if you need help, I will help you." I knew he meant this genuinely and I was really grateful to Hussein for his advice and friendship.

As it turned out, the next day, I had arranged a driver to take me to Aswan which is about a 3 hour drive from Luxor. I didn't get a great vibe from this driver and on the way, I discovered his intentions were less than honorable. Now I was stuck in the car with this man, I didn't really know where I was, I wasn't sure what to do or if I did call anyone, would it make things better or worse? Ironically when Ahmed and Hossam took me to the airport in Cairo for my flight to Luxor, Ahmed became concerned for my safety when I told him that I would arrange for a driver to take me to Aswan and he said "I think you would be better to go by train". He was right and I now wished I had followed his advice.

The day got worse. The Philae Temple in Aswan is located on an island. You purchase a ticket for the Temple and then you find a boat to take you there and agree a price with them. I was the only tourist on the jetty when a young man eagerly offered to take me, but at an exorbitant price. Now I was stuck again as there were no other drivers available so I rang David and asked him what to do. Following his advice, I went back and argued with the driver threatening to report him to the Tourism Police for over-charging when an older man intervened and gave me a fair price for the boat trip and gestured me to go with this man. The driver was not happy with me, I didn't want to be on his boat and as we docked on the island, he swore profusely to another driver which I must say is not something I have ever seen an Egyptian do. Relieved to be off his boat, I did wonder if he would come back to collect me in 1 hour.

Once on the island, I made my way to the Temple. Eventually a large group left the area known as the Holy of the Holy's and I was left alone to meditate and connect with this ancient sacred site. I probably had 5 minutes to myself when I became aware of a guard hovering behind me. When I opened my eyes, he told me to follow him and I thought 'here we go again'. As I hesitated, wondering if I could trust this man and against better judgment, he encouraged me to follow him, which I did. Before long, he put his hand out for baksheesh (a tip) and angrily I told him to leave me alone. I must have given him one of 'those' looks because he ran after me apologizing and then I knew he was worried that I would report him to the Tourism Police. I encountered more of the same behavior from 2 other guards and I eventually found a place where there was no-one and broke down and cried. I just wanted to be left alone to honor and enjoy these sacred holy sites in peace. As I cried I started to hate Egypt and the men here, vowing never to return. But really, it was not Egypt or the men here, this was all about me and how I was not dealing with the situation and standing in my own power. Hussein's' advice was so accurate; I was not standing my ground with these men.

Later that day, I met Mustafa who is an owner of a shop in the hotel where I was staying. I ended up spending a long time talking with him and another shop owner Muhammad and eventually shared my day with them. Mustafa became upset for me and actually apologized for the experience that I had which was really touching especially as it has nothing to do with him. He wanted me to have a nice experience of Egypt and set off to bring me some tea. Meanwhile, Muhammad an older man who was of Nubian descent told me that he does not have very much money, but that he is 'rich' in family and friends. He knows what's important and he is very happy with his life. He touched my heart too and I was grateful for their kindness and hospitality. They helped me to let go and be at peace with all that happened in my day, opening heart to all the beautiful humble people there are here in Egypt, that I love so much.

I left Aswan to return to the Bahariya Oasis in the Western Desert. I love being in the desert, there is something so magical about it. In particular, I was keen to camp overnight in the White Desert National Park which is a few hours' drive from Bahariya. This however, was not meant to be.

In the original itinerary, I had requested to camp in the White Desert and it was included in the price. Then I made some changes and without me noticing, it was removed. Soon after arriving in Egypt, I discovered the error and went about arranging it once again. It was all set and the day we were planning to camp, a wild sandstorm blew up making it impossible.

My local Egyptian guides did take me out to a place in the Black Desert and the energy was so incredibly powerful that I was in awe of what I was experiencing. It really was wild, the sand horizontal most of the time with these massive wind gusts making it swirl like mini tornadoes. With the sand being so fine, it gets everywhere yet the pure raw energy of it was amazing to experience. My local driver and guides were not as excited about this as I was and if we could have got a tent up, I was more than happy to camp overnight. But it was impossible and so we had to head back to the hotel. Ironically, this was the third time I have tried to camp in the desert but for whatever reason, it was not meant to be and the greater purpose of why this is so, has not yet been revealed to me.

Back at the hotel, Peter the owner had arranged seating for his guests. I was to be seated with Michael for dinner. Michael was a young German tourist who had just arrived in Bahariya. He had driven from Cairo and was quite shaken by how hard it was driving in the sandstorm and nearly had an accident. Michael was really interesting to talk to. He is a designer and he told his boss that if he wanted to keep him, then he needed 2 months unpaid leave every year. He organizes 2 trips, one with friends and one alone where he has been exploring Africa. On his travels, he meets the local designers and experiences life through their eyes, which he journals with the intent of publishing it into a book. He also takes his learning's and applies them to his own design work. It's a real win/win.

We shared our experiences of Egypt and I came to learn that he gets hassled just as much as I do because he is single. He also had some great advice about negotiating and gave me a completely fresh perspective on it. And he left me with the wisdom that despite some of the challenges I experienced on this trip, he said "you have learnt from them and they will never happen to you again". Michael was like a breath of fresh air, an inspiring young man rich in life's experiences and so connected to his purpose and his path.

These sandstorms bring rain and we had a taste of it in Bahariya. Mostly though Cairo experienced big downpours over a few days which is unusual and Ahmed told me that as a consequence of the storm, they had a very brief experience of snow in Cairo. When they drove me back to Cairo, I was amazed at how clean the air was as normally it is what I call 'black air' which essentially is very polluted. The rain and wind had definitely brought a major clearing and it was around this time that I learnt of the earthquake and tsunami in Chile and came to realize that everything is ONE, we are all connected and this is all part of the greater Earth changes.

This time when I left Cairo to return to New Zealand, it was the first time I did not cry. Egypt is my spiritual home and I now know that I will always return here, that there is always a calling to come home and not only do I belong here, but that I am welcomed here by the Gods and Goddesses of the Temples that I am so connected with.

When I was back in New Zealand, one of my friends in Egypt sent me a wonderful text and as I was on my way to my art class, I said I would create a painting for them. Later when I reflected on the painting, I came to realize there was an important message contained within it. The painting is reflective of the heart and the message is "to honor your heart, listen to what it tells you" and mostly, when you are faced with life's challenges, "follow the wisdom of your heart". I feel this is a message for all of us.

Maa Salam.

About the Author

Joanne (Jo) Hutchinson was born in Auckland and resides in New Zealand with her daughter Hannah. She holds a Master's Degree in Business Administration (MBA) and has an extensive corporate background in sales, marketing, customer service, leadership, managing and developing people. Her breadth of skills and life experience make her multi-talented with a deep understanding of both people and business, and leadership from the heart.

Her passion has always been people and seeing people grow and develop into their full potential. She led a major New Zealand company to be values based which provided her with the understanding and insight of what was truly important in her own life. This led her to make significant changes in her life and was the start of a significant period of personal and spiritual growth.

Honoring her spiritual gifts and talents, Jo founded her own companies; Great Spirit New Zealand and Great Spirit Journeys Ltd. The essence of her work is about helping people to ignite their inner spirit. Her work now involves teaching people the 'spiritual art to life and work' which is based on understanding the concept of purpose which is the 'why' behind all that we do and founded on the timeless spiritual laws. She shows people how to integrate these teachings into everyday life, so that we can create our dream life and live life with meaning, love, joy, peace and prosperity.

Jo is a spiritual teacher that channels many Beings of the Light including the Ascended Masters, the Ancients, the Gods and Goddesses and the Angelic Beings of the Light. She also takes people on spiritual journeys to the ancient and sacred sites in the world with her signature tour being Ancient Egypt. And she is an artist.

For further details on Jo's work, workshops and tours, please visit; www.greatspiritjourneys.com